Flowers

The art of relationship, love and desire.

and Honey

Julie Tenner

CHANGE
EMPIRE
BOOKS

First printing, 2020.
Printed on demand in Australia, United States and United Kingdom.

Edited and designed by Change Empire.

ISBN   978-0-6450217-2-1 (ebook)
         978-0-6450217-3-8 (print)

Published by Change Empire
www.changeempire.com

CHANGE
EMPIRE
BOOKS

Dedication

For my children:

may you one day find this book
on a shelf of wisdom,
pick it up and open the pages.

May you feel my beating heart
yearning to whisper truths to you.

May you smell the baked goods and
hear the laughter we shared
over so many years in the
very space I wrote this book.

May you tuck its wisdom into your pocket
of golden nuggets and carry it forward
into creating the life of love
you were born to experience.

I love you.

Thank you for sharing your life with me.

Forever and always,

Mum xx

How to use this book

You can read the book from start to finish, or you can choose your own adventure!

To choose your own adventure, simply decide the destination you want to get to, or the desire you crave answers for, and head straight to those sections, listed below:

Feminine

Unsure what the feminine is in you and your partner ...

3   The flower (feminine energy)
5   The feminine (flower) gifts
8   Open or close
11   Open your petals, flower

Why being in your feminine can be hard ...

15   Owning your feminine can be hard to picture or imagine if you've been trained otherwise, can't it?
19   The flower's rejection of her feminine
22   Attachment, not truth
26   Family, the first place a flower learns
31   Don't short-change your needs
33   Rule-breaker

Unsure how to get in your feminine …

37   Feminine practice is different to masculine practice
38   A further rejection of your feminine flow
40   Say "yes" to your body, not "body, you are wrong"
42   What if I'm afraid to feel?
45   Numbness and trauma

How to establish your feminine practice …

47   Relaxation of the feminine body
48   Amplification
53   Amplification is NOT performance
54   Adornment is worship

Masculine

Unsure what the masculine is in you and your partner …

61   Mountain (masculine energy)
62   Penetrate or withdraw
64   Single focus
68   Beginning to see differently
71   When your interruption from his single focus does not feel good
74   When your interruption from his single focus feels good
78   The 30 second pause
80   Working with the mountain's single focus
82   What single focus can feel like for a flower witnessing it
86   Competition and challenge

Feel uncertain whether he can 'handle you' as you try to open or 'change the game'

89   Density
92   Learning how to let him see, hear and feel your truth (not a diluted version)
94   Learning your energy communication
99   You're always training him

Desire

He's in his feminine but you want to be

107 Holding feminine polarity
109 Polarity as it already exists within your relationship
113 Leading

Creating intense 'spark', chemistry, desire and attraction within your relationship

117 Where does polarity exist in humans?
120 Polarity practice
122 His presence matches your energy
125 We all outsource what the relationship doesn't provide

Relationship

Knowing how to tussle with you (for mountains also)

131 Where it gets tricky
134 We think we're seeking his passion, but really we're seeking depth and presence
136 She craves your presence (masculine practice)
137 Flowers test, mountains align

Communication and disagreement upskilling

139 Bypassing intimacy, stop assuming, start sharing
142 Get on the same team
144 Uplevel your communication
148 Get targeted

Conclusion

If you're ready for more after this, head over to julietenner.love and connect with me.

The suggestions and practises described in this book are **not** rules. You are not trading one set of rules for another. These are *offerings* and *knowledge* from a lifetime of self-work and spiritual practice, and 17 years of working with women, relationship and intimacy.

You do not have to follow anything word for word, but if you're willing, what you'll find here is the missing key. The piece that a part of you has longed for, but not known how to access. This is the missing ingredient in a relationship built on trust, honesty and equilibrium. You can have an intellectually, spiritually and emotionally equal relationship – but without energy polarity, you will *not* have sexual chemistry, desire and passion. This book paves the way for taking your relationship to the next level, to a place of intimate union: where we can love as equals and opposites, as two parts of a whole.

Information is power. You do not have choice if you do not *know* your choices. This book presents you with choice and power. Do you want to take it?

What to do when you're lost

Pick one step or work your way through all five:

1. **Go as fast as the slowest part of you.**
   Resistance is one step beyond closure, towards opening. You are moving in your own divine timing. Trust that.

2. **Just feel.**
   Every time you feel, something, anything, you're in your feminine. Once you feel something, ask yourself "how could I feel this even more?" or "how could this feel even better?" Revisit the section "Amplifcation".

3. **Follow your pleasure. It will always lead you to what you desire.**
   Begin simply with "what do I want right now?" and give yourself *that* in every moment you ask it. Journal on it if that feels better. Set a reminder on your phone – ask yourself this question every hour until you learn a new way of being in the world.

4. **Book in some receiving time.**
   Receive a compliment, a massage, a hug, a rest, a hot kiss. Practise receiving (instead of doing), and you're practicing your feminine energy.

5. **Communicate with "I feel" and try for fewer words and more body-feeling.**

About the author

Julie Tenner is The Pleasure Nutritionist. A mother of four and an experienced facilitator of deep women's work, she is a naturopath, nutritionist, herbalist, counsellor, doula, intuitive bodyworker and Divine Feminine and embodiment leader who teaches women how to love wider, feel safe in surrender and open up to their untapped magnetic power.

The daughter of a yogi, Julie has a lifetime of spiritual practice and over 17 years of experience working intimately with women's physical, emotional and relationship health. She believes pleasure is the missing ingredient to women's wellbeing and their ability to radiate their love and light out into the world.

Julie creates safe and sacred space for women and couples to explore more of who they are and how they love. A sage and guide in women's mysteries, she infuses deep knowledge with humour in a distinctive combination of heart and soul, bringing awareness to dynamics and healing that lead the way for deep relationship transformation.

A born storyteller, Julie weaves old world magic with modern savviness, captivating audiences all around the world through facilitation of women's circles, ceremonies, events, online learning and training programs, in addition to co-hosting her podcast, *Nourishing the Mother*.

A self-proclaimed pilgrim of love, Julie will revolutionise the way you relate to yourself and the ones you love, bringing deeper connection and richer intimacy.

Gratitude

Thank you to all the women who shared their stories with me; it is an honour to tell them. Reader, I hope you, too, find yourself among their wisdom and feel the power of such diverse lived experience. May we all grow and learn from the wisdom of the stories women carry.

Soul-deep gratitude to Bridget Wood, who I met in 2013 at a playgroup. From that day forward, my heart and soul have known an alignment for which I will be forever grateful. Thank you for you, your belief in me and all the incredible heart-rich, soul-deep work we've done together. You light my heart on fire.

To all the magnificent podcast listeners who feel like best friends; knowing you were on the other end of that mic was often what gave me the fortitude to keep going. Thank you.

To the lovers and members of my work as it exists now: thank you for sharing your hearts, souls and most potent life experiences with me. Your ongoing support and vulnerable participation has been a profound honour and has shaped many of the words channelled, not only into my courses, but also onto these pages. Thank you.

Endless gratitude to Carlie Maree, without whom this book would not have been written. You saw me at a time I couldn't see myself. Thank you for you, your guidance and your courageous heart. My soul revels in watching you flourish.

Heart-aching, soul-opening gratitude to the magnificent human I've had the honour of intimately sharing 20 years with, through arguably the greatest life transformations humans know. My husband, Nick – who, as he reads this, will feel deeply uncomfortable with owning the light he himself embodies and has shed on mine. I couldn't have done this without you. I wouldn't *want* to do this without you. Thank you for your love, your unyielding support and your belief in me. And thank you for *all* the experiences that led to my wisdom. I love you, deeper than my humanness can comprehend.

Jules xx

Foreword

This book is a temple. Please leave your self-berating or minimising dialogue at the temple door. You can pick it up again on the way out, if you want. This is a temple of feminine practice. These pages contain ancient teachings combined with the rich experiences of my life, as well as all the stories of women who have come before you. This is a book of Her-story (history as told by Her). You will hear what you've never heard before. Sometimes it will be hard. Sometimes it will feel like the scripture missing from your life. Heartbreak and heart opening are sacred. So let's worship together – ego and criticism can wait outside. Come into the temple with me ...

Understanding Energy

You are a mix of feminine and masculine energy.

There are women who are mostly masculine energy; there are men who are mostly feminine energy.

There are women who are mostly feminine energy; there are men who are mostly masculine energy.

There are men and women who are a relatively equal balance of both masculine and feminine energy.

There is no right or wrong, good or bad – but without opposite energies, there is no attraction or magnetism.

Your energy is completely separate to your biological sex and sexual preferences. There are homosexual men who are very masculine. There are heterosexual men who are very feminine. There are lesbian women who are very feminine. There are heterosexual women who are very masculine.

This magnetic attraction (magnetism created between masculine/ feminine energy) exists within heterosexual and LGBTQI relationships. One person within the couple will animate more masculine energy and one will animate more feminine energy. Either partner can take up a stronger masculine or feminine polarity, whether in a queer or heterosexual relationship.

Hopefully by now, you realise that energy and sexual orientation do not necessarily go hand in hand – that the forces of attraction are universal to any interaction between a masculine energy and a feminine energy, rather than between genders or sexes.

Regardless of your sexuality and gender, the majority of the time you will either identify more strongly as someone who embodies masculine energy or someone who embodies feminine energy, and you will seek the opposite energy in a partner (regardless of gender or biological sex).

Traits associated with masculine and feminine energy likewise are not associated with biological sex or gender. Today we know people of all genders can have any combination of these traits and energies. While feminine and masculine are completely separate to biological sex and gender, the words feminine and masculine can be helpful in describing two different and opposing ways of being, so we will continue to use them throughout this book, interchangeably with the terms Mountain, to describe masculine energy, and Flower, to describe feminine energy.

Masculine

Alternative words to describe the same thing:

- Mountain
- Him
- Man
- God
- King

Traits and attributes:

- Consciousness
- Would rather emptiness or nothingness to feeling
- Seeks freedom and release from tension
- Presence, stillness
- Direction, decisiveness, leadership
- Right, wrong
- Perfection attainment
- Goal-focused
- Able to stay on track, complete tasks
- Desires "to take" sexually
- Giving and penetrating energy

Feminine

Alternative words to describe the same thing:

- Flower
- Her
- Woman
- Goddess
- Queen

Traits and attributes:

- Energy, light, love, life force
- Fullness
- Feeling, emotion
- Chaos
- Going with the flow
- Surrender
- Nurturing, nourishing
- Bodily pleasure
- Movement
- Intuition
- The flow of love feels great
- Desires to "be taken" sexually
- Receiving and allowing energy

In simple terms, if you find yourself doing everything on your own, setting goals and achieving them no matter what, you're animating more masculine energy; this is the energy of "pushing" and is also referred to as "giving" and "penetrating" in this book.

If you love to go with the flow and don't worry about the future because you trust life will bring you what you need, you're animating more feminine energy; this is the energy of "pulling" and is also referred to as "receiving" and "allowing" in this book.

The teachings within this book are about the art of energy and the flow of desire (magnetism) through an understanding of the masculine and feminine polarity within yourself and in your relationship.

The majority of my work has been with women in relationship with men, so this book is written with women in mind and uses gender-normative language. However, the content is written specifically for the partner who identifies more as feminine energy, irrespective of gender or genitals. All are welcome here. Please don't get lost in my hetero-normative, gender-based wording – it is far less important than understanding the energies as they exist within you and your lover.

Maybe your relationship was great in the beginning, but now it's just bland, mediocre – more a function of Family Inc. than a meeting of lovers. Perhaps you feel resentful or undesirable, or as though lust has left your life, refusing to paint the colours of the vibrant relationship you once imagined. Maybe it's a beautiful life of best friends; there's so much love but just no spark.

I promise you I understand. I've been where you are, but I also know it's not where the story ends. I've found a pathway to unrelenting desire, outrageous intimacy and the deepest, most profound love in a 20-year-long relationship to one man, with four kids and two businesses in tow. I can help you. I promise you it's here, on these pages – the stories you were never told, the understandings that were never shared with you – but sometimes it's going to be uncomfortable.

Let's talk about this discomfort first, so when you experience it, you know exactly where to return. Our beliefs create our behaviour. Our repeated behaviours create our conditioning, reinforcing our original beliefs, and on the cycle goes. We are creatures of habit who enjoy certainty and control. The moment our beliefs are challenged and what used to be "known and true" becomes clouded, we lose the certainty and control we thought we had, and it can feel destabilising. It is this moment you have two choices:

1. Reject my words, argue the point with all the justifications and knowledge that have informed your current behaviours (and relationship), and stay closed to the possibility of change.

Or

2. Entertain the possibility, open to a new way of being, try out ONE tool with curiosity and see what happens.

I hope you choose the latter, because like thousands of women before you, you will discover something incredible. You get to have everything you want, with the man you want to have it with. Truly.

Understanding magnetism and polarity

This book's sole purpose is to make you aware of your energy, the effect it has on you and your relationship and the power you have to change it at any moment. Once you achieve an understanding of the energy you're "putting out" into the world and into your relationship, you have a better understanding of what is energetically "coming back" in, and why.

Before we begin, you've got to understand the impact of your energy and what happens when you're in a certain kind of energy. The moment you understand this cause and effect, you get to decide what you want to be and what you want to attract in response.

So, let's begin with a bit of science (stay with me). Physics is the study of the relationship between objects, forces and energy. Physics explains the basic forces upon which our entire universe is constructed, including gravity, magnetism, electrical charge and the way things move, us included.

When an object (or person) has extra electrons, it has a negative charge. When an object (or person) has extra protons, it has a positive charge.

Protons have a positive charge, called positive energy or positive pole. **Electrons** have a negative charge, called negative energy or negative pole.

Objects (or people) with opposite charges are always attracted to each other. Positive charges seek negative charges. Negative charges seek positive charges. The mechanics of these forces of attraction create electrical currents, magnetic attraction or repulsion, and are the foundation of all natural forces within our universe.

Two sames repel or are neutral.
Two opposites attract.

The attraction between masculine and feminine energy completes an energetic force. It's not that another person "completes you," it's simply that an energetic force seeks balance and the best way to "balance" is to come into union with its opposite, creating a type of "stability."

It is this balanced state, achieved between two opposite and equal forces, that creates magnetic attraction. When you put two masculine energies together there can be conflict; when you put two feminine energies together, there can be conflict. But masculine and feminine together create an effortless magnetism.

You have an energetic charge, and in response to that there is an energic charge you are attracting, repelling or coming into neutrality with.

No different to the magnetic pull between a positive and negative magnet or the electrical charge between positive and negative ends of a battery, desire and passion are the result of a force of attraction, created when two opposites come together.

Hence, the more "same" the energy is between you and your partner, the less sexual chemistry (attraction) there is. The more opposite the two of you are, the greater the sexual chemistry (attraction) is.

The problem is this:

- Love contracts distance and seeks to make the other "the same," resulting in neutrality or repulsion between intimate partners.
- Desire requires "distance" (opposites). The greater the difference (opposites), the greater the current of attraction and desire.

Does this mean you can't "be the same" and have a great relationship? No! It means you CAN have both; love AND desire, friendship AND attraction. You *can* flip between the two energies depending on what you want.

A bestie to hang on the couch with? Cool. Be "the same" and sexually neutral and *enjoy* it!

A stimulating intellectual equal to debate with? Cool. Be "the same" and *enjoy* the energy created from "bouncing" off each other (repulsion) or take pleasure from there being no sexual chemistry distracting your mind and thoughts (neutrality).

A husband who looks after the house and kids with an overwhelming amount of love, care and tenderness? Cool. He'll be in his feminine, offering feminine gifts, and consequently you'll be in your masculine, free to kick-ass, make lists and nail your next business goal. *Enjoy* it!

A completely equitable household and family life? Awesome. You get to have that too! Enjoy equality: it's beautiful, but largely sexually neutral.

If a relationship full of love and sexual neutrality is what lights your heart on fire, enjoy it! It can be absolutely beautiful – but then this book is not for you.

But, if you desire to *be* desired, to be fucked into oblivion, to be craved, seduced and surrendered in a rapturous rendezvous with the love of your life, then energy neutrality is a form of death – and this book *is* for you.

If you desire a man with a strong masculine energy, a man who leads, directs, organises, makes decisions and enjoys ravishing his woman ecstatically, you need to learn to manage your energy to be in feminine receiving energy. Strong men can handle powerful women. They're just not *attracted* to masculine energy.

If you desire to be the boss in your relationship, and you desire a man who is more willing to do what you want, who has a beautiful calm, compassionate, caring energy, who listens and lavishes you with his feminine energy, then you will need to learn to manage your energy to be in masculine giving energy.

If you desire a completely equitable relationship, where all jobs and responsibilities are shared evenly, where there's love but no sexual attraction, where you're best friends who enjoy hanging out over stimulating intellectual conversations and are the best of colleagues on the Family Inc. team, then you both need to learn to manage your energy to be in neutrality, neither of you taking up a strong energetic force, but rather maintaining a relatively equal balance.

The laws that govern this magnetic polarity exchange are the same laws that govern our universe. What you put *out* reflects what you get *back*. This is the Law of Attraction at its most basic. The interesting thing with any manifestation is that it requires *you* to *first* send out your energetic "wish," doesn't it?

Have you ever manifested something you didn't *first* feel, think about, say out loud, send out to the universe and continue dreaming about?

I'll bet after you "sent your wish out" and declared what you were seeking to "call in" from the universe, you placed that beauty on a vision board and began to consider how you could begin to make steps towards it becoming a reality. You see, universal forces respond to intention. The basic math of manifesting is:

INTENTION + INSPIRED ACTION = MANIFESTATION

Without inspired action, a wish remains a wish. It is the same with our energy (how we feel) and our relationship (how we're felt by our partner).

The women I work with generally adore the concept of manifestation. When it comes to their dream house and the next year's money goals, they're *all in* for "putting their order in with the universe," removing any blocks they have to it "coming in" and working towards becoming the woman for whom that reality is possible.

Yet, when it comes to relationship, they'd rather defer their personal power and responsibility and say *He needs to give it to me. I'm deserving*, followed by pouting and cursing when what they get back doesn't match the wish they had in their mind.

There are no winners or losers here. The moment you go first, the universe responds. This is the law of manifestation. It is the same in relationship. You go first, you put your energetic "order in" with some inspired action steps (which gets to feel wonderful for you!) and what you get back changes, instantly.

Any attachment to "all the hard work is mine" negates the profound influence you have as a force of attraction and instantly closes your energy up – less energy = less response. If you only *slightly* believe you can have what you wish for, does it come? I'll bet the times the law of attraction *has* worked for you are the times you've manifested with energetic abundance and total belief. You got into alignment with your desire, and it arrived as you ordered.

It is the same with our partners. If we choose to stay with our previously conditioned beliefs and habits, this can feel heavier, more burdensome and impossible. I want you to claim more of who *you* are and learn what you were not taught, so you can live a more vibrant and energetically ecstatic life, where *you* get to choose how you feel and what you experience in your relationship.

But please don't go into this wanting to create a change in your partner. This book is about *your* path to change. Your path to empowering your feminine and understanding the energetic polarity play with the masculine. This information has the power to change your life, relationships, work and finances. **This is about you.**

This book is written *for* you. If I were writing a book for masculine mountains, it would be different. Our world already champions the masculine; it's not usually the energy women need help to cultivate. So this book is a tour guide of the energetic differences and a tool kit for those of you wanting to claim more feminine space.

Sometimes, this may feel as though there's a lot of responsibility on you to "fix" your relationship, and you may find yourself asking "but what about hiiimmm???"

I don't see relationship as something that needs "fixing." I always see the function in the dysfunction. We are always in dynamic and responding to energetic forces. These are always orchestrated *for* your growth, though growth is often painful. Our greatest revelations are often borne of our greatest pains. Without a framework to apply this understanding, pain can cloud your vision, insight and understanding. Sometimes, it can be hard to see the wood for the trees in our own dynamics. Whatever your spiritual practice, this is the time to look towards it.

Does this mean there are not mountains that need "a good talking to?" Of course not. We are all flawed humans, and in every dynamic there is something for each of us – but I didn't write a book for a couple. I wrote this book for a flower so she can find *her* way home to *herself* and in the process spark tremendous magnetism. What she does with that power and magnetic attraction is up to her.

Consequently, there are a few sections in here specifically for mountains (masculine beings – see "Knowing how to tussle with you"), but the majority of the information is for flowers (feminine beings). With great power comes great responsibility, and sometimes responsibility can feel like burden. At these times, just put the responsibility down, girlfriend. Come back to enjoying the life you've created, in the body you have. Spend time with "the good things in life." Flow a little more. When it feels full of burden, you're in your masculine – time to get back in your feminine, for **you**. I promise you'll feel instantly better.

This book is my homily. When you get lost in scripture, come find me. There is always a way for this to land in your body and life. You can join my "study group," Honey Club, or any of my learning programs any time you like. You don't have to do this alone.

Let's explore together. Bring your desire for more with you.

> *It wasn't for me, it was for my daughters.*
> *I want something different for them, something more.*
>
> *But I didn't even know that more existed.*
> *It was an idea, an unanswered question, a curiosity, a longing.*
>
> – Cathy

Introduction

You're here. You made it. I'm so delighted you did. I wrote this book with you in mind.

In the words of one of my dearest friends: "I feel like I'm curled up in mother earth when I'm with you." Come, curl up in my energetic lap and let me tell you the story of *your* heritage.

Let me share with you what has been kept from you.

Let me show you another way of being and belonging to this world, to relationship and to sex.

Let me tell you the truths that whisper through your bones, that pulse through your heart, that sit in your hips and upon your lips.

THIS book is for the woman *sick* of denying her power.

For the woman who can no longer tolerate mediocrity in her relationship or in her life.

Who loves her man deeply and wants more.

It is NOT for those who have their relationship nailed and who find their intimacy effortless.

It IS for the woman who feels as though she spends most of her time running in her masculine, winding up exhausted, dissatisfied and fed up with how she feels within herself and her relationship.

It IS for the woman who knows she has this thickness that sits at the front of her body, preventing her from flowing openly with love, from giving what she knows exists within her to the ones she loves and to the world.

It IS for the woman who wants to know the music with which her own body sings.

It IS for the woman who knows she's a beautiful, strong being all on her own, but who still craves to swoon into surrender with a partner.

It IS for the perfectly imperfect woman whose relationship still feels difficult, however many years she's into it, who has seen beyond the veil of infatuation and dances with learning her embodiment and deepening her intimacy.

It's for those of you just like me.

I'd love you to learn men and women anew. To throw out every pre-conception and formed idea you have been taught and to embrace a new reality.

It's not that "he can't meet you" or "he's not man enough" or that the man you desire is not present in the man you love.

It *is* that you have come to believe you need to be your own man, and in this world of universal laws, there's no room for him to be what you already are.

In a culture that prizes the masculine traits of strength and rationality, goals and production, while also minimising the feminine gifts of beauty, nurturance and emotional flow, it can be hard to find, much less claim, your connection to your feminine. It is in these pages that this changes.

The relationship you crave, the man you desire to be fully taken by, appears as if by magic the moment you claim your innate feminine and learn to balance your own inner masculine.

Your feminine is the gift of invitation and magnetism. The Goddess draws towards her that which she desires. You, too, will be able to do this by the end of this book. This book is the law of attraction in relationship.

You can have a kick-ass business, be a boss-babe, a rock-star CEO or plan your kids and your household like an absolute badass. But you *also* get to experience your natural feminine flow and recharge your magnetic energy.

Take the world *and* allow yourself to *be* taken. Relish and experience every delight this world has for your mind and vision *and* every delight it has for your heart and body.

This is not the world of either/or. This is the world of "**and**" ... be that *AND* ... have that *AND* ...

I have been in relationship with my man for 20 years. We've had four kids together. Before I learnt how to ignite passion in a long-term relationship full of all the normal life pressures, I decided that he was incapable of meeting me and I:

- Disconnected
- Looked for other outlets
- Castrated him for "not getting it," for being an insufficient lover or desiring to find any other solutions

And **I decided** *he* was happy with mediocrity – until I learnt I had it all wrong.

And now, today, this "regular Aussie bloke" (as opposed to the uber-conscious unicorn one) breathes me open every time I have rising tension in my body, without my asking. "Breathe with me," he says. Two breaths in, I'm a hot, juicy mess.

This doesn't "just happen."
I didn't just "find a good one."
I'm not "lucky."
This. Is. Created.

You've tried demanding, complaining and ice-queening him, only to find yourself more hurt and unmet.

There's another way, and it gets to feel delicious for both of you. Enough of mediocrity.

Enough of putting up with rubbish connections and bland sex. You were made for more.

Love and desire are not the same. They are not cultivated in the same way.

Love *contracts* distance.
Love craves belonging and sameness.
Desire craves *distance*, energetically.

Opposites that ignite chemistry.

Once you understand this, the path to an electric relationship becomes clear, and you are in the driver's seat.

As we embark on this journey together, I want you to hold close the words of my toddler and revisit them any time you need a reminder of the amount of power you hold within you:

> *I am not stuck.*
> *I've got this.*
> *Fire shield out.*
> *I've got you, baby.*

Let's go. Together ...

Feminine

The flower (feminine energy)

The flower is the representation of feminine energy in this book. The feminine is literally energy and can be seen as light, felt as love, heard as music etc. The feminine is "everythingness," because it is energy that forms everything: all matter, all form, us and the world.

The feminine within all of us has strengths that we will call "gifts" or "traits." These are the gifts of nurturance, sensuality, receptivity (feeling), receiving (allowing in), empathy and emotionality. When we experience the feminine in ourselves or another, we feel lighter. We feel truly heard, seen, felt and deeply touched. We relax, our mind softens, tension and stress melt away and we drop into the present moment. We feel what is here in this human body to be felt, and we experience rejuvenation and revitalisation. Our feminine IS our ability to experience bodily pleasure and the present moment.

The feminine within all of us is expressed through movement, creative flow, dance, play, empathy, nurturing and care-taking, sensuality, intuition and feeling.

The feminine within us *loves* to feel. The greater the feeling, the greater happiness for a flower. The removal or absence of feeling is felt as pain. Withdrawal, stonewalling, absence of feelings or feelings diminishing are all mini-deaths for a flower.

A flower craves to be "filled up" (a masculine craves to "empty"): romantic comedy or drama movies that make her feel more, foods that are strong enough to make her feel something, shelves that are full, walls filled with memorabilia, candles, music, colours, layered fabrics, wine, poetry, gatherings, parties, celebrations – anything that makes her feel more. More is always better than less for a flower!

A flower's ability to "be filled" and experience "fulfilment" is dependent upon her ability to *receive*. By receiving love/energy/attention, your feminine energy is "filled up," resulting in her feeling fulfilled.

You receive every time you allow love and energy to enter your body. This can be through receiving a massage or a pedicure; letting your lover's words or your child's laugh touch your heart; enjoying a nutritious meal a friend cooked for you; or feeling rejuvenated by witnessing the horizon over a vast ocean. Your ability to allow yourself to be "looked after" (rather than looking after) *is* your ability to receive and will be directly proportionate to the level of feminine energy you pulsate with.

When you allow yourself to receive in all its fullness, you don't resist or reject; you don't try to avoid "letting it touch you." You fully embrace this moment and surrender to everything it has to offer. You are fully present – not holding anything back, just opening and feeling.

It's no different to receiving a massage. Your breathing, relaxation and surrendering to this moment and to the masseuse allows them to penetrate your muscles and all the layers of tension more deeply. The more you allow yourself to receive, the deeper they're able to penetrate you (and your muscles); the more fulfilment your feminine energy receives, the more rejuvenated you feel.

Flowers adore opening and receiving, to let *more* in and let *more* out, in a constant motion of flow. She suffers when energy is clamped down and held on to. When her body is full of tension and stress, energy cannot flow, and *not* flowing is pain for a flower. In many humans, it is this accumulative tension and lack of "flow" that leads to loss of ease in the physical, mental or emotional body.

Energy and feeling are bliss for the flower.
More.
Even when what she has is enough, more feels *better*.
An open heart.
An open body.
A current of love.
No end-game, just more fullness experienced now.
Bliss for the flower ...

The feminine (flower) gifts

This ability of the feminine to bring a human into contact with the pleasure found in their body is why she's been so greatly prized throughout history. Behind every great man is an even greater woman, right? Often, it's because she's his "secret weapon." It is through the experience of being around her that he's able to "tap" into inspiration only found through awakening pleasure pathways in the body, where the thinking mind recedes and the soul can sparkle through. You might recognise this as "flow" or "an artist's flow" or "channelling."

It is an aspect within all of us. It's why we love a motivational leader or will pay to "plug in" to someone else's energy. It is feminine energy that enlivens us. What we do with that energy individually, once it has been "woken" within us, is our own art, but in each and every moment, it is a blessing from "the Goddess."

Just sit with this a moment longer, because this is often a sticking point for many women seeking to embark on this journey with me. SHE rejuvenates. You. Me. Him. Her. She enlivens your very cells. You feel more awake, happy just to be alive, sparkly and in love, calm and connected. The feminine energy within all of us is our source of replenishment. Our masculine will keep running until we've got nothing left. But our feminine – she will look after us, nurture and nourish us, let us know what we need to come back to wholeness and joy. The moment we feel her, we're blessed. Literally. Like a dip in the immortal spring of life. Like the Dali Lama laying a blessing upon your head. You are instantly changed.

Think about the times you've walked into a gathering and you're met by a woman who is so friendly, so gloriously open, her smile so wide and her eyes so fixed upon you with delight, that you feel welcomed home and are transfixed. Whatever you were thinking the moment before you entered evaporates instantly. She feels like sunlight and golden honey. Like a summer breeze, her presence and energy brush through your body, and you feel instantly better. Welcomed. Invited. Wanted. Lit up. You want to be around her more. When she offers a catch up, you can't wait. While you can't pinpoint what it is, she's just glorious to be around. Around her, you feel better. Maybe more inspired. That's the *She*.

Worshipping and loving the feminine for these gifts is not an objectification of women. These gifts come from anyone who animates this energy within them. It is an energy within each and every human, though the degree of its animation and free-flowing gifts will differ between each of us. She is in men. She is in women. It just so happens that humans animating more feminine energy will take on more stereotypically feminine ways of looking and being because they are *flowing* with more feminine energy! That is not an accident.

The feminine is ever-changing, flowing. She is everything round, soft and sensual. She delights in curves and swirls and movement. So you will find her in places that animate this more thoroughly, human forms included. The more a "vessel" is designed to flow with feminine energy, the more healing and rejuvenation is available individually, collectively and on this planet.

We can love and adore women for who they are AND we can love and adore women for their power of *She* (feminine/Goddess energy or animation). Loving her for her feminine gifts does not diminish who she is or what she's here to accomplish.

We can open up more feminine energy into any area of life in which we wish to seek more revitalisation. We can want to open, invite and relish more feminine energy within us, our relationship, our family life or finances. "Anywhere" we're ready to be in a state of receiving and rejuvenation, rather than pushing and driving.

A woman who animates a large amount of feminine energy is literally a blessing. To anyone. To all of us. Man or woman. This is not a lessening of who that person is, man or woman. But if you are in a relationship with a masculine partner, *your* feminine is one of the things he can't consciously understand or intellectualise but that he adores about you and is compellingly transfixed by.

When you animate feminine energy, he comes to worship. Literally. Like a bee to honey, he comes towards you to receive the blessings of being around this energy. Same as any of us who have chosen to sit at the feet of a guru, watch a dancer or see a musician live. WE receive a transmission *from* someone who flows with feminine energy and it changes who we are in that moment, and therefore what's possible in the moments that follow.

To adore the feminine is to adore everything life touches and to relish every experience this life has to offer. I'm a devotee, and I will teach you how to open the feminine within you, revitalising your relationship, rekindling desire and rejuvenating your energy.

Life will never be the same and by golly it will *feel* better!

Open or close

When in your feminine energy, these are the only two "options" (traits): open or close. Flower energy opens and closes (masculine energy penetrates or withdraws). When you're receiving, you're open, fully allowing in, fully flowing inward and outward. When you're closed, you're "switched off" and shut down; nothing gets in and nothing gets out.

It is equally as important to know what "opens" you as it is to know what "closes" you.

For instance, some flowers need heat to open; they need to feel warm. Good to know.

Others need music or sensual delights like candles or scents. Easy to consciously put in place.

For some flowers, it's the dark that opens them. For others, it's the security of certain words spoken by her lover.

For some, it's touch. For others, it's being watched and adored, before touch.

For some, it's being served a drink, having kids put to bed, taking a shower totally on their own.

For others, it's space to go quietly inward, to find the spark inside her heart or body first, before she shares it.

For many flowers it's movement, dance, embodied and unscripted flow.

> *For me, it's morning meditation followed by spontaneous poetry writing.*
>
> – Tui

What blooms you open, flower? What are the activities you *know* make you feel open, flowy, loving and deliciously soft in your energy?

I once had a woman in one of my programs who recounted her own grandmother telling her "God is in the dishes." She said she never understood it until now; when she was unconsciously moving, when her conscious mind took a *step back*, she was *free* to channel, to receive energy and messages from the divine.

For grandmother, granddaughter and many women I've met, God is indeed in the dishes, or dancing in the kitchen.

For me, it's the shower, in music that opens my heart or body and in an endless ocean horizon. For others it's …

> *The sunrise. The ocean. The dewdrops on barren winter trees. Cool fresh mountain air in my lungs. My babies laughing. Cuddles. The smell of my kids. Flowing on the yoga mat. Breathwork that takes me to bliss. Red roses, the ones that smell like heaven. Music that makes me cry. Nuzzling into someone's neck. Candlelight.*
>
> – Claire

In the light filtering through the trees.

    – Emma

God is in the ocean for me. And in my babies' sleeping faces.

    – Carlie

Move about your day asking yourself, "does this make me bloom?" Listen for the response of your heart and body. Do you swell, swoon and bloom? If not, good to know! You just found something that closes your bloom. If you have just discovered something that makes you bloom, wonderful! How can you include more of this? Be willing to play and discover, and if it doesn't light you up, give it up!

Do you need to open to your world with new and refreshed eyes, with curiosity to discover what opens you? If life were a banquet and you were invited to dine upon all of it, what would you choose to try?

> *It's definitely not shiny yoga on my behalf but when I practise it, it feels like I'm weightless ... There is so much less tension in my body when I give myself the gift of presence/exploration/surrender. I know I have only taken the first step and at times it can feel wayyy "too hard" (cue anger, why me, retreating, I don't have time, if he didn't then I wouldn't ...) but those practises dancing, writing, sounds, movement subtleties and then suddenly I can look back on these small steps and feel pretty good about it!*
>
>   – Sarah

What blooms you open, flower?
What closes your bloom?

These are important answers to know as a flower.
These are important answers for your lover to know.

Open your petals, flower

A flower feels ecstasy when she's pulsing with feeling and is most at home when she flows with love, most inspired when she follows her heart's calling. All of her energy is expanded when energy flows through, and from, her heart. Even if you have internalised shame at such a statement, it is still the truth at the centre of you, still the answer to your exhaustion and the key to your magnetism.

Your heart yearns to be seen, to be touched, to be felt, to be moved, to be opened deeper than you can open it yourself. Instinctively you know this; you crave to be *met* by your lover in a way you cannot meet yourself.

> *It always shifts so much quicker and ends in bliss. I love those times when I've had a big emotion come up and without words really let myself feel it and show him and he has come up behind me and sat with me, put his hands wherever I needed them, and held me through it. That luscious masculine still strength.*
>
> – Allyce

> *For me it's during sex. He will often somehow intuitively know what I need to bring me deeper into myself and into my body.*
>
> – Nicole

Secretly, perhaps, you long to surrender to the vast unknown of your heart, energy, the universe and love. To let go of your thinking mind, your masculine ways of being, directing and achieving and flowing *into* life itself. When you surrender to this energy, it will guide and animate your purpose, your power and your potency. It is the crux of your creativity and expression in this world.

Energy received, felt and expanded *is* bliss for the flower. There is no "end-game," just now, just this moment, just the energy present, and She does not differentiate between energies. Whatever is needed for her bloom and for bliss to be felt is what she surrenders to, what she "births" into the world.

> *My biggest revelations and growth have been around feeling more. Opening my heart and feeling everything without making it wrong, shutting it down and doing what I always do – run to my room to cry. I would never let him see my pain. I didn't want him to see he had hurt me or I was hurt by something he did. So I would run and cry in the bedroom. Compose myself and walk back out like I was strong. Tough. Invincible and he couldn't hurt me. I know this stems from childhood wounding. Witnessing this I'm re-training myself to stay. Feel. And not run. And the hardest for me, let him see it.*
>
> – Nicole

Claim your luminous energy flower. It will be your medicine and your guide. You are an energy centre entirely unto yourself. Like the sun, you *luminate* from the inside out, generating your own light. This is why you are so precious. This is why men have given up countries, fortunes, family, life, in order to receive *your* illumination. There is *no more* precious resource than this feminine luminous light. It IS life. You are precious, flower. Even if you believe you are more solid than something so delicate. You. Are. Life.

> *I have been playing with my feminine polarity while away camping this week. Husband just said, "You seem really feminine this weekend; it's like you are glowing" (not words he would ever normally use, and certainly not in a camping context). I asked if there were any particular moments he noticed that, and he listed*

off the EXACT times when I was really trying to open myself into that energy. Amazing, they really do notice and feel the energy change! So very grateful for the things I have learnt here already!

– Meagan

I am life. You are life. We are life. The feminine within all of us is the energy of life. It is more and more of us glowing with light that will heal this planet.

Owning your feminine can be hard to picture or imagine if you've been trained otherwise, can't it?

Our culture celebrates and enhances masculine traits and gifts, and tends to diminish feminine traits and gifts. In centuries past, this has been our stereotypically gendered society. Women look after kids, beauty, decoration, cooking and care giving. Men dictate society, industry, wealth, culture and law. Anyone who got anywhere in this masculine world was either a man or animated a large amount of masculine energy. We came to associate success with the masculine, and political weakness, intelligence inferiority and economic disempowerment with the feminine.

The only way for women to have a voice was to fight on this masculine plain as equals. More than equals. In order for women to gain power and have a voice, they had to be better men than most men.

It is to this feminist movement and all the women who sacrificed children, safety and life in order to rise above that I owe all of the privilege and entitlement I now freely enjoy. I love these women. I adore their courage. I admire their bravery and honour the radical shifts they created individually and collectively. And it continues to be a much needed movement in order to close the pay gap and leadership at the highest levels.

However, being a woman does not make you feminine. There are women who are just as masculine as any male leader. She may in fact be the most masculine energy in a room. Whenever we animate a large amount of masculine energy, we will continue the narrative of goals, success, drive, superiority/inferiority, winners/losers, black/white, less feeling, more mental conscious thought. Being a woman does **not** automatically make you a devotee of feminine energy, nor does it mean you worship, honour and adore the gifts and traits of the feminine, though without them your life will never feel fulfilling.

You can be a woman, a feminist, a female-empowerment leader, and **still** you can be *feminine rejecting*. You can believe that in order to "get ahead" you need to be less "feminine." More hustle, less feeling. More drive, less presence. More ambition, less flow. More push, less allowing. Do it yourself, because no one is doing it for you. Get what you want. Take it. It's *yours* for the taking.

Do you turn your nose up at the woman who loves to nourish her home? Who dotes on her partner like he's gods-gift? Who wants nothing more than a lifetime devoted to her children? Who is the hottest thang in the room but relies completely on a man to look after her? Do you judge, minimise or ridicule her?

Do you believe motherhood is a pause in life? That, somehow, it's "hiding" by "withdrawing" from life and the hustle? That you're not sharing your brilliance or your gifts?

Do you think if you are appreciated for your beauty, you are not appreciated for your intellect?

Would it be a certain kind of death to be dependent on a man?

You're "more than that," right?

You can be a feminist **and** you can be feminine rejecting because you don't *really* see the true nature of the feminine. You don't see her blessings. You don't see her gifts and magic in the world. You only measure this world based on a set of principles into which the masculine indoctrinated you. You don't really honour Her. You champion gender but not the feminine within us all, this earth included.

In centuries past, your survival has been dependent on your ability to animate masculine energy, but now this world will only be healed when we bring the feminine traits and gifts into equality.

This is the type of equality I wish to see in the world. Not gender-based; it's too simplistic. Energy-based equality. It is the power of this feminine-rising within all of us, gender irrelevant, that will heal this planet and all the people in it.

But let me step it back.
That can feel too immense, can't it? Or perhaps too far off?

Let's talk about you. Just like the feminist wave, change starts with you. Change is always with the power of one.

If mind and rationality have been championed over feeling and intuition for your lifetime, it will feel hard to relax into your feminine. If you've spent a lifetime never able to depend on anyone outside of yourself, if you've needed to fight for survival, then "just receiving" can seem naive.

If your wanting or desiring was never allowed or was labelled as "greedy," it will feel complex. If "more" has been a dirty word for you in your lifetime and lineage, then the mere concept of opening up to your feminine can have you feeling uncertain.

I wish to allay your fears. I wish to soothe your heart. I wish to soften your body. You can have this. You *get* to have this. It is your birth-right. But the path towards it does not look like hustle. It looks like pleasure. Truly.

Whoever told you "no pain, no gain" was running in their masculine. The feminine says, "the more pleasure I feel, the more influence I have."

If you feel closed and shut down, sick of the hustle in your life, business or relationship, then you're ready for change, and this book can help you do that.

You might read my words and, I hope, feel a craving to move forward from the centre of you (opening) and possibly feel like it's unreachable (closing). I want you to know, if you can feel the desire for something, you can have it. You don't yearn for something that is not possible for you.

This doesn't have to be hard. In fact, it gets to feel *good*.

As a rule of thumb, when in the feminine, if it feels good, you're doing it right!

The moment you feel (anything), you're in your feminine. The moment you feel *even* better than you did a moment before, you're in your feminine power. The more you surrender to that feeling, the more you receive – and guess what?! The more you feel, the deeper your feminine polarity.

To live in your feminine energy is to feel into your sovereignty. It is not to be perfect or succulent all the time. You are not one-sided. It is to be devoted to your heart first and foremost and to be aware of your energy. And it is to remember that a queen never rules alone. She can do hard and great things *with* a support crew, please find the women who will fan your flames and support your journey into embodied living.

The flower's rejection of her feminine

The path of spirituality, I have found, is in feeling and removing all the obstacles to feeling. I am the daughter of "an original" 1960s hippie-yogi. I grew up with brown seed bread, nutritionally packed muesli, Kombucha, electromagnetic deflectors and a father who did a 1–2 hour yoga practise at 5am every single morning. Without fail. "White bread soon dead" is still a catch-cry of his that rings in my head.

I learnt commitment and self-discipline from him. I learnt breath work with him. I practised stillness. I could meditate with the best of the transcendentalists by the age of 13. I cultivated nothingness. It's part of why I have such an exceptionally healthy masculine that in many ways is easier for me to "sit in" than my feminine.

However, I also was never very good at it! I was like the kid in class who was an exceptional student on paper but partied hard outside. I felt. I flowed. A visibly feminine body. A separation grew inside of me, one that took a good 20 years to reconnect.

This perfectly, pristinely, healthy mountain-yogi died of cancer. He too was exceptional at smoothing down, or away, feeling. Sometimes, our feelings can eat us up from the inside out if we keep them locked away.

A lot of flowers keep their feelings locked away and live with a heavily guarded heart. Like Pandora's box, we're terrified of what might emerge when we open it.

Maybe as a young flower you were told your inner truth was wrong – that the way you felt, your ability to read people around you, was incorrect. Maybe you were taught to trust your rational mind, outside direction and culture more than your heart, feelings or intuition.

Perhaps as a young flower, you were trained to see how the feminine heart was unpredictable, crazy, wild and untamed. Perhaps your appetites and desires were wrong and would lead you astray. Perhaps you read the stories of asylum incarceration or listened to the men in your life talk about "crazy women." Perhaps your mother was emotionally unpredictable and "crazy."

Perhaps you were raised by a mother who *forgot* she *was* a flower, staying so still and stiff and tight-lipped, never allowing *herself* to have needs, never being directed by something other than her own logic.

> *For so long I've forsaken my feminine by appeasing in relationship. Revealing my hurt, then backtracking for the sake of the other, preventing their hurt. Trying not to be too much. Suppressing my anger.*
>
> – Megan

Perhaps your emotions were too big for your parents as a young flower; you grew to accept *you* were *too much, you* needed to *flow less* to receive love. Maybe you came to believe the best, most lovable flowers are those that *do not* flow at all. Maybe your brother got all the attention, so you set about being better and achieving more than him.

Perhaps you learnt the aspects of you that "flowed" were irrational and not to be trusted, that the display of them resulted in ridicule or love's withdrawal. Both are deeply painful experiences for a young flower.

I come from a family of very strong women. Marriages where the women make all the decisions and have all the masculine power, while the men all sit quietly and do what they are told.

While this has taught me to be strong and independent, it has been hard as an adult to learn to accept help, to "receive" love from others, or to let my partner take the lead.

The concept of women being powerful in their feminine energy was never role-modelled to me. When I experiment with feminine energy now, it still feels dangerous!

    – Meagan

Maybe the mountains in your life took pieces of you like you belonged to them. Maybe you grew to mistrust your own flower nature and did your best to look like a mountain, so the other mountains would notice you less, because feminine attention for you equalled danger and pain.

When "she" wanted pleasure, I said no, because I felt I wasn't allowed to, I only knew pain, never really experienced pleasure."

    – Pamela

Maybe masculine traits were more celebrated in your family, or you needed to be smarter or better in order to receive love, attention and validation.

In my teenage years "she" was let loose and it was clear that I couldn't achieve all the success I wanted in the world while "she" was running the show, so "she" had to be put on a leash and shut right down.

> – Allyce

Maybe your saw your mountainous father as untrustworthy. Perhaps you never had a mountain to trust. Perhaps being *your own* mountain was safer than finding one outside of you to trust.

With varying efficiency, flowers can smother or cut off their flower-nature. Instead of constantly being open to pain, you close against what you perceive as the cause(s), and the flower within you withers.

The degree to which you reject your feminine will be the degree to which you over-compensate and animate your masculine in its absence.

I had to reject all feminine to provide for my family.

> – Cathy

Attachment, not truth

Feelings are the superpower of the feminine, so why do we dislike them so much? Why do they sometimes feel destructive or unsafe?

The feminine is *all* energy. She not *only* is the culturally accepted notions of kindness, light, romanticised love and gentleness but also represents the natural forces of the entire world. Sometimes She's a summer breeze, sometimes a typhoon.

It is our human experience that dictates whether these forces (energies) are "good" or "bad." In their truest sense, they are neither. Everything is neutral until we attach meaning. Meaning is informed by our cultural, familial and personal experiences; these create our beliefs, which then inform our reality and experience (remember this cycle?).

It is worth spending a short amount of time considering the attachments you have to certain emotions (energy in motion) that would inhibit you from feeling, allowing or expressing them (feminine rejection).

You may share attachment stories similar to these women:

Anger

It's ugly. Bad. Frightening. Out of control. Shut it down. Don't touch it. Be sad instead.

> – Carlie

Uncivilised. It was naughty to feel it as a kid in my house. I could be sad, but angry was bad behaviour. You're not allowed to display such strong emotions. Go away and come back when you've regained control.

> – Wendy

If I get angry, I've lost my composure and I've failed.

> – Mel

Love

Hurts. Is painful, isn't real, doesn't exist.

> – Melissa

Is mean, unsupportive and scary.

> – Julia

Is for girls with their head in the clouds.

> – Sarah

Sadness

I'm trying to manipulate him with my emotions.

> – Wendy

Crying = being weak, soft, over emotional. No one will like you if you are sad. Your feelings repulse people. Go away and come back when you've got a smile on your face.

> – Cathy

You have no right to be unhappy, because you have so many blessings in your life. You must be ungrateful to be lonely or sad.

> – Kate

Happiness

You are likable, lovable, friendly.

> – Brooke

If you're happy, you're about to experience a low. Don't get too happy about being happy. Calm down your joy. You have no right to be so happy.

– Angela

Sometimes I feel the need to hide my happiness to be relatable. When I was young the one that was always happy was annoying and had her head in the clouds.

– Lorna

Agreeable

Don't rock the boat, don't question, accept the leader.

– Cathy

Don't put other people out.

– Kat

Your needs are not as important as others. You are selfish when you choose yourself first.

– Sandra

Vulnerability

Is weakness, don't cry, man up.

– Pamela

Don't show emotions, swallow it and move on, don't express how you feel, shut up, you have no voice, you don't matter, hide.

– Rachel

You're not strong enough, you get ridiculed or punished.

– Sarah

Sexy

Stop being such a slut. Why are you so flirty? You must be man-deprived. Who are you trying to impress? Stop trying so hard.

> – Pamela

Women are not your friends. They hate you. They're suspicious of you.

> – Pip

Men think you want to have sex with them.

> – Sophia

Which attachments do you think hold you back?

Family, the first place a flower learns

Hopefully, you've considered what attachments you have to feelings. Now, let's look at what attachments you have towards the feminine that run wider and deeper. In order to transcend our relationship with our own feminine, we must re-form the attachment to our feminine that our culture has hidden from us, that centuries of torture, death and suppression have cut us off from.

First, there are larger cultural beliefs and conditioning that have influenced how you think and feel about your feminine, because they have influenced how your family think and feel about the feminine. There is an ancient part of you that still carries this knowledge and these wounds from centuries past. On a deep (and sometimes "irrational") level, there's a part of you that fears death or "tribal" rejection and isolation. If you were to own the full power, light and attraction of your feminine energy, what might happen? Likely it doesn't feel very safe.

You may find yourself thinking:
What if I'm too much?
What if I attract too much attention?
What if I attract attention, and I'm unsafe?
What if women reject and ridicule me?
What if I'm cast out?
Attraction = manipulation
Lust = death ...

A few women in my groups shared their internalised beliefs:

> *I can see I've learnt from my mum (without her even aware she's been modelling it) that being feminine and softening makes me vulnerable and weak.*
>
> *– Lauren*

> *Women were meant to engage, flirt and intoxicate, not be FRIGID. But only as entertainment for men, not to own a deep desire of their own because women might then be promiscuous and a SLUT. The body should be desirable BUT only for the pleasure of men, not in pursuit of your own pleasure and don't enjoy looking good, being appreciated, praise etc. or be cut down.*
>
> *– Tara*

What beliefs about the feminine do you hold within *your* body and psyche that are from your culture?

Then there is the part of you carries the stories of the women in your lineage – your grandmother and mother most potently. You existed as an egg inside your mother's ovaries, as she herself grew inside the womb of your grandmother. The stories they felt, the experiences they had, have an imprint on who you are and how you see the world. Sometimes the "stuff" we struggle with may not even be our own. It's worth knowing about the experiences of your mother and grandmother, especially while they were pregnant, and seeing if there is any correlation with your current struggles or beliefs and their stories.

Compounded upon culture and family programming are the experiences of your own lifetime. How you think about and experience men, women, relationships and sex are learnt by watching those with whom we grew up. We are continually "blueprinting" our care-givers views (felt and expressed) on relationship, intimacy and sex.

For instance, you may share some of these beliefs:
- Sex is for baby-making only.
- If I flirt, I'm leading him on, shut that down, it's dangerous.
- Men only want you for sex, and once they've got that, they leave
- Don't give in to temptation, to the devil. Don't give in to desire. There's a line and once you cross it, there's no coming back. Sex outside "the rules" brings loss and shame.
- Women are responsible for men's arousal and control (or lack thereof); "she brought it on herself" victim blaming.
- Women who need men are weak. You don't need a man.
- Your beauty means girls and women won't like you; you'll have no friends.
- If I'm not nice, I'm a bitch.
- I must provide what he needs, regardless of how I feel and what my body says.
- Men are incapable of love and intimacy.

- Men are an inconvenience, scary, unnecessary, selfish, not to be trusted, let you down and do not tell you the whole truth.
- Men determine what I can and can't do, if I am good or bad, if I am worthy or not.
- If I'm not looking after others' needs, I'm selfish.

How were men, women, relationship and intimacy role-modelled to you? What have you "blueprinted" (and play out) in relationship dynamics? In sexual relationships? In intimacy (or lack thereof)?

On considering this, a few women in my groups shared the blueprints for intimacy they grew up with:

> *Dad wasn't around, mum feared men from abuse. I never witnessed her interact romantically with a man.*
>
> *– Megan*

> *I learnt my well-cultivated masculine and "I can do everything for myself/I don't need a man/men are useless and more hassle than what they're worth" from my mum. So the only "functional" relationships I observed were my grandparents, who slept in separate rooms and bickered at each other all the time; and friends' parents, who of course only show you the "always happy" part of the relationship. I actually feel like I have no idea what a healthy, functional relationship looks like.*
>
> *– Amelia*

> *Parents trapped in a loveless marriage, separate bedrooms, money arguments and negative enabling behaviours. Just mediocre coexistence.*
>
> *– Sarah*

Sexuality wasn't discussed. I learnt about periods from my older sister. Pregnancy was the worst of all sins; if you come home pregnant, I'll kill you. This was before I even really knew what sex and attraction were, or had an interest in boys, so sex was definitely a forbidden taboo.

> – Can Dee

My parents never demonstrated any sexuality, sensuality, intimacy, attraction, or attention towards each other. They are happily married, 40 years plus. It seems a combination of the generation that doesn't talk about anything, and the religious background that means it's not discussed or displayed.

> – Cathy

I learnt to fear the Male, he was the boss/ruler, not to speak unless spoken to, (fear of punishment) most times I was wrong if I didn't do it his way (I would get punished), act/do the way he wanted me to. All have played out in my relationships. I was raised as a Jehovah's Witness, so no sex before marriage, marry within that religion, which played out as rebellion and I used sex as a bargaining tool or would give it freely and hurt myself as punishment.

> – Pamela

However you learnt it, most women carry a degree of separation and fear from their feminine and learn how to cloak it so it is not seen, felt and noticed by others – until one day, we can't find it *ourselves*.

Don't short-change your needs

The feminine does not say, "Oh no, I couldn't possibly."

She says, "Oh! Thank you so much! Yes I will, thank you!"

When stepping into your feminine, it is important to take ownership of your needs. Not so you can be the only one who knows them or can give them to you, but so you have a pulse on *your* energy and what She needs to become vibrant again.

If you only ever allow yourself to meet your own needs, you will never feel fully fulfilled; there will always be a vague distaste or disgust of every man who cannot meet you (because you don't ever let him).

If you only ever wait for others to anticipate and meet your needs, if you only ever receive when someone else gives you permission, you may be waiting for a very long time.

If you believe you are here to serve and sacrifice for others, that your needs are not as worthy as others, that someone needs something more than you do or that you don't deserve "x," you will end up shrivelled up.

Feminine energy, like auspiciousness, is attracted by and magnetically drawn towards an energetic match. She does not visit barren, harsh lands where she is disrespected. She simply leaves. And you wither. "Crops" no longer grow; people are treated harshly; empathy, compassion and the gift of giving are absent. The "lushness" of life no longer exists.

When you short-change or skip out entirely on your wellbeing, you end up taking it out on the ones around you. You are no longer in a place of abundance, acceptance and receiving; you are now starving and will fight to get what you need.

Unmet needs, stacked and shoved down, sooner or later become *neediness* that we project or "vomit" onto our lover (or loved ones), only to feel doubly hurt and rejected when they struggle to meet the force of our need.

Neediness becomes suffocating (the opposite of the freedom masculine energy craves) and has a penetrating energy about it (masculine energy) that will cause him to withdraw. If you are pursuing, telling or demanding, you are meeting your partner in a masculine energy, while they are also in theirs; the only outcomes are penetrate or withdraw. Whoever has the stronger masculine energy will win. The other will withdraw and recede. It's the same as any animal species on this planet.

This dynamic is shifted the moment you take self-responsibility for your energy and remove all the blocks to it.

You are the pulse of life-energy within your relationship and family. Your energy is paramount to the health of all, this world included. Your needs are not selfish. They are self-honouring. They are worshipping.

What do you need to be self-honouring and feeling abundant again? How can you ask for what you need, ask for help or give it to yourself (receiving)?

Rule-breaker

Oh, flower, you have SO many rules. So many ways to coerce yourself into pushing through, to keep going when you've nothing left. The tension, constriction and deprivation can at times be intolerable, and still you will make yourself stay. You can survive. You can withstand. You can keep hustling, even with nothing left in the tank.

Maybe it's terrifying to rock the boat, create disturbance in others, put others out. Maybe you were trained to be a "good girl" and it's abhorrent to consider feeding yourself first, instead of last. Maybe you were raised by a flower so concerned with herself, you learnt to meet others' needs first because your needs weren't wanted or allowed. Or maybe you're equally repulsed at the thought of being "anything like her," such that you will starve or run yourself into the ground just to be the opposite of her.

Maybe all the rules allow you an ability to relax? A paradox, yes, but a coping strategy. Rules give you a sense of control. If "chaos" is scary or you don't trust yourself to "know when is enough," you'll create rules to hold yourself to a standard or to avoid pain.

If we're full of fear about a perceived future, the way to avoid entering that fearful situation (and any associated pain) is to control as much as you can. Believing you can steer yourself and everyone else *away* from pain. The greater the perception of chaos, the tighter the reigns of control. This is a classic masculine energy manoeuvre.

Maybe you were praised, valued and seen for everything you DID and achieved, so achieving and lists are really important to you, and without direct and visible targets, you feel lost and invisible. Motherhood may be a battering ground for you, an endless list of tasks that never ends and that no one recognises, in a culture that doesn't value your work.

Whatever your "set-up," in response you learnt to create rules for yourself. So. Many. Rules. **Rules like these women created:**
- You can have three squares of chocolate, but not four.
- You can have leftovers, but not a gourmet lunch.
- You can wear track pants all day, your girls can float in beautiful dresses.
- You're allowed "this many" minutes of rest, but not "that many."
- You can't go to bed until the dishes are done.
- You can't swear in front of the kids.
- You can't watch a movie, read a book or do a course for you during the day when the kids are home.
- You should try to always look the way you did on the day you got married; don't let yourself go.
- Your pleasure is based on his approval of how you look.
- All domestic duties are performed by you, without help, quickly, efficiently and to a high standard, and then you also make sure everyone else is happy, cared for and attended to before yourself.
- You can't have sex with kids awake during the day.
- You can't kiss in front of the kids.

What are the rules you have for yourself, your partner, the couple, parenting ...?

> *I realised all the rules I had once I was married and had children weren't even mine to begin with, yet I'm trying to follow them.*
>
> – Bronwyn

How can you experience the thrill of breaking them?

Perhaps you are afraid of the ravenous nature of your feminine appetites and desires, so you feed "the beast" *just* enough to stay alive, but not enough to *thrive*, because what might happen?? Would the needing and wanting *ever* end? Would you become so consumed and gluttonous you'd destroy your parenting or relationship?!

All rules hide untapped potential, energy and intimacy. Whenever we break "the rules," we experience a rush, the thrill of novelty. All our excited neuro-chemicals come dancing to life; it's the hormone cocktail of desire and infatuation.

You can ignite curiosity and spark desire any time by breaking the rules you have! Change routine into excitement, and you've got a recipe for instant chemistry.

It would be a wonderful date to both list your rules, individual and shared, and then discuss creative ways you could break them **together**. Promise you'll feel like "naughty teenagers" again.

For instance, I never used to let myself hire a babysitter so we could have a day date. It was a rule I had. What sort of mother was I if I left my kids in care for something other than work? Our dates became possible only at night, and I was always tired at night. The day I decided to change this, I began with two hours of sitting for the sole purpose of enjoying daylight hours together. It was pure magic! I felt rebellious. I felt like a dating lover again. I remembered how much I enjoyed his company and our banter. Now it's my date of choice; day dates feel *way* more nourishing for me than night dates.

Here are some other rule-breakers:

> *Now, if the situation calls for a "for fuck's sake," then that's what comes out. And guess what, no one died ... I realised it's just a word and how good does it feel when you say it! Fuck, fuck, fuck, fuck!!!*
>
> – Brooke

> *I still carry the load of domestic duties more, but that's also because I don't ask him to help. As soon as I ask him to help or allow him space (and don't override him in the task) it gets done, without me having to ask!*
>
> – Bronwyn

I wonder what you're going to do and allow in ...?

Feminine practice is different to masculine practice

Traditional yoga (as opposed to feminine-embodied yoga), meditation, EFT, hypnotherapy and cold therapy are all wonderful examples of masculine practice. They are practises that seek to cultivate soothing states of bliss, of nothingness, directed towards calming energy and emotion, feeling less instead of more. Separating mind and body.

This is wonderful if you need more masculine energy! If you are a flower out of balance, if you tend towards more hedonistic, present-minded indulgence with no future focus, direction or goals, completely dependent on others to look after you, you may indeed need some more masculine cultivation.

If you are an empath who has no control over what you feel and will feel *for* others to your own detriment, feeling before you can understand *what* you're feeling, or have a bleeding heart that gives out beyond your resources, you may indeed need masculine cultivation.

But. If you are already well resourced in the masculine energy department, already a natural leader, completely tapped in to the bigger picture, able to keep your mind on the prize no matter the hurdle that comes your way, full of drive, motivation and hustle – you likely don't need further masculine cultivation.

What you do need is some feminine flow. Some allowing and receiving. A cultivation of your force of attraction where hustle is not needed.

It's all about balance. Likely you will want both energies within a healthy relationship and individual, and an ability to "flip" into either energy depending on what is required or wanted by *you*.

More attraction and magnetic pull? Get in your feminine. More future focus and planning? Get in your masculine.

You get to decide which energy needs building within you.

A further rejection of your feminine flow

From all the yoginis I have worked with over the years, what I have come to know is this: they are often the most "skilled" at repressing and suppressing their anger. So focused on "their light," calm and contemplation, so practised at awareness, cultivating "dealing with" or "smoothing over" dark emotions, they **bypass** practice and **yoga-over** pain instead of deeply feeling and expressing. Often they find yoga a way to "cool" their "feeling pain," which is a marvellous skill set for cultivating a stronger masculine (necessary for wholeness), but to create balance, you *then* need to be willing to advance beyond "awareness" (avoiding feeling) and into "feeling" more.

Meditation, yoga and exercise can be used as healthy expressions, AND they can be used to disassociate from feeling. This is what "spiritual bypassing" means. The idea of transcending feeling states and "evolving above" the need to express certain (very useful) human emotions that you may judge as negative, like anger and jealousy.

"Observing feeling" is very different from experiencing feeling. Meditation, traditional yoga and exercise are all absolutely important and can definitely be part of a healthy process of working *with* your emotions, but not when they are used as escapism from what you are being called to feel and transform.

Exercise and spiritual regimes are only detrimental when they affect your ability to surrender. We are meant to be powerful *and* we are meant to be soft. Bypass can be applied to anything we use to disassociate from feeling and to look outside ourselves to fix "the thing," rather than facing the deep inner pain: shopping, eating, screens, excessive work ...

The path is always *through*. Not over, under, around, locking up and throwing away the key. Your body and its responsiveness is *on the way*. If you are working so hard at "keeping the beast locked up," **you'll lock up your desire and expansive sexual energy, too**.

If you need feminine cultivation and practice, put in place a daily practise (see the next section on "How to establish your feminine practice"). Actively create moments throughout your day to experience your bloom, flow and feeling.

Say "yes" to your body, not "body, you are wrong"

We are working on creating greater alignment, not disconnection. Your body is working *for* you, with you. It is only conditioning that's taught you otherwise. On this path to awakening your feminine, where there has been suppression for a long time, once the river of feeling begins to flow again it can feel more like a torrent.

In saying "yes, I will listen" to your body, she can want to tell you all the things she's been holding, all the "backed up" feelings that have been waiting for their chance to release. You may find you meet a lot of sadness and tears. Does this mean it's not your path? No.

Instead of "this is bad," what would it look like to say "this is opening and release"?

What would it be to say "yes" to your body and whatever wishes to come through her?

What would it be say to your inner little girl, "yes my darling, it's okay to feel, you are welcome here. I will listen"?

Please know tears are a sign of release. A sign you're no longer "stagnant" and holding emotions back like a dam, but are once again flowing as the river of life. As you let feelings flow in, feel them for a while and let them go, just as a river does. Tears will carry with them the release of all the stagnant stress hormones you've been holding. Let it be a blessing and feel it as a cleansing and relief.

If we stay as the dam and only allow a small "trickle" of emotions through, we end up experiencing only a middle grey in our life. Feeling unfulfilled. Feeling dull and lifeless.

Emotions come in pairs: two sides of a coin, a light and a dark emotion. To feel rapture, we must know deep surrender. To feel ecstasy, we must know hurt. To feel open, we must know closed. To awaken joy, we must know depression. As soon as you cast one as "bad" and reject it, banish it to the locked basement, she takes her lighter sister with her. They are a pair. The river stops flowing and you live in the "middle grey."

The more open a flower is to receiving energy, the more she feels it and lets it *be* felt by others as it dances through her, the more alive she feels.

> *I have learnt to grieve, rock, moan and ugly cry in front of him, let him see me, let him feel me. It was brutal, first time I've ever cried properly. It was exhausting. But it changed everything.*
>
> – Cathy

What if I'm afraid to feel?

Feeling may be so foreign to you, or so laden with story, that you're not even really sure how to enter your feelings.

You may find yourself carrying similar experiences to these women:

We were taught to never show emotion. Hell, I didn't even know what that was, I was such an empty shell.

    – Pamela

Suppress all emotions or they will take over. If you want to perform well at work no one must see your emotions.

    – Niomi

In this case:
- Go gently. Go as fast as the slowest part of yourself. Anything faster will shock you backwards, and we want to make your expansion safe.
- Despite what you may have learnt, your feelings are not bigger than you, because they *are* you. *You* get to choose how much, how fast. Let yourself play with your edges and let feelings seep into your body for an additional five seconds at a time. Be willing to see what you can do and what you can master.
- Seek professional help to work with your own nervous system regulation and ability to process if you have a history of trauma.
- Consider a belief you're ready to let go and try these exercises:
    - Begin to look for where the opposite is true. Who represents this opposite belief? You can look to social media, friends, podcasts or books for this inspiration.

- Get curious: ask women you see who express this trait or action how they see it. Share the belief you hold and seek to dismantle it. Ask them what *they* think about this belief, how *they* see the world differently. Be willing to see the world as they do.
- Create an affirmation for yourself reflecting this new belief you're wanting to "install."
- Ask yourself: what actions could I do daily, weekly or monthly to stretch this belief?
- To "lock in" this new belief, what are the pattern interrupts you could do when your old belief rears its head?

For instance:

"You can't have a successful relationship and be a successful woman."

Where did I pick this up from?
- Mum, Dad, school, social media boss-babes I follow

Where is the opposite true?
- Julie and many other women I follow on social media
- My friend Sally
- My mentor

How do they see it?
- Julie: "Not true at all. I believe the more you feel full, expressed and vibrant, the better your relationship and business get. The more feminine energy, the more abundance in all areas."
- Sally: "No. I love my husband and my kids and my work. I don't sacrifice pleasure for any of it!"
- Mentor: "Belief is all that holds you back."

Affirmation:
- "The more I let my energy and inspiration flow, the more abundant my life and relationship get."

Pattern interrupts:
- Whenever I notice this thought process, I will instantly do an act of pleasure for myself until I feel my energy rise.
- I will actively put in place daily steps for accessing my feminine.
- When I kick-ass in business, I will allow myself to fully swoon and feel ecstasy both bodily and emotionally with my man when I'm home.
- When I feel like he's not meeting me, I will work on being an energetic match for what I seek and keep "in practice" until I receive exactly the quality of exchange I'm seeking.

Lastly, put yourself in a community of women who support your journey. We are the product of the people we spend the most time with. If you're seeking change, consciously create experiences where you can be in the company of those who embody this way of life – online groups are included in this. Have a space you can energetically plug into, bounce ideas off, challenge the status quo and awaken new possibilities within you.

Other women will be your greatest allies on this journey, I promise, even if some of us have learnt to mistrust women. To avoid them. To seek the company of men instead, under the guise that "men are easier. Girls are too bitchy."

The way you have learnt to reject the feminine *outside* of you is a mirror reflection of the rejection of the feminine *inside* of you. One of the greatest wins of the patriarchy was to pit women against each other, as happened in witch hunts and in the fight for survival when women were unrecognised as citizens and were without any power.

Your ability to stay safe and attached to men was an act of survival. Men have known for centuries that when women come together, they are more powerful individually and collectively. Women's power amplifies in the presence of other women. Keeping women separated, mistrusting of each other and towing a "pleasant" line is a sure-fire way to avoid any "nasty women," isn't it?

Be a rule-breaker. A system shaker. Love the women around you. *Let* them love you.

Numbness and trauma

What exists in your body is *on* the way to your healing, not *in* the way of it. Numbness and pain count. You may find yourself subconsciously choosing to feel nothing over feeling everything.

I'm yet to meet a woman who doesn't have stored trauma in her body. Trauma, as I see it, occurs when someone experiences too much, too soon, too fast, regardless of context of the experience. Avoid playing the "trauma Olympics"; trauma *is* trauma in the body. It is irrelevant on a feeling level whether your experience was "worse" or "better" than another's. Too much, too soon, too fast creates an emergency cycle in your body, one that may not have been completed yet and may feel as though it is "triggered" on a repeat cycle. The pain of entering these sensations can feel so overwhelming that you may have learnt to disconnect instead, resulting in dullness or numbness.

Your numbness is your body's attempt at protecting you. Love her for that. Be with your numbness and be open to any messages she has for you, before you desire to "move on."

When you've fully felt your numbness, as with any emotion, it will fully dissolve and a new feeling will arise; often, for the feminine, it will be anger or pain before it is pleasure or ecstasy.

Please know, anger hides hurt and hurt hides desire. If you're unsure what you want or desire, you may need to "remove" what's blocking it and be with some anger or hurt first.

> *I have trouble feeling anger. At the same time I have always thought I don't have desires. Have no clue what they are. Wow. I get it now. My desires are all under the fear, hurt, and anger!*
>
> – Nicole

Even with numbness, how can you connect to it right now?
How could you more fully feel numbness?
What does numbness ask you to do?
What does numbness need?

Often behind numbness is deep pain, which was so painful for so long that you disconnected from it, so you could live without constant pain. Please remember, from pain and awkwardness can come ecstasy. You're not breaking. You're birthing a new version of you.

Relaxation of the feminine body

Tension will stop the flow of energy. Tight, tension-filled muscles and organs cannot flow with energy. Relaxation of the feminine body allows energy to flow. A feminine body flows, ripples, bends, sways, just like a flower. She is responsively moved by the energy within and around her.

A body trained to be masculine becomes still, angular, rigid and hard. The longer you spend in your masculine, the stiller your body will become. The stiller your body, the less energy is present. The less energy, the less feminine polarity.

For energy to flow, for feminine embodiment and pleasure, soft is the way. Relaxation is your friend. Stop holding your tummy in, contracting your solar plexus filled with insecurity, closing your heart to protect it.

In this culture, we are taught tough, tight, taut is better, but the first place to begin any feminine embodiment journey is connecting with your body and breathing so fully you can "breathe-out" any tension. Breathe deeper than you currently are, however deep or shallow that is right now. Use your breath to consciously relax your muscles, particularly down the midline of your body. Breath is the queen of the body. Let her hold court.

Your relaxation is the key to your energy-flow.

Soft, relaxed body. Front surface of your body soft. Soft parts, soft (tongue, throat, breasts, belly).

Midline of your body feeling open.

Heart open and informing your direction.

Heart leading, hips following, OR hips leading, heart following, any direction you take.

Let your head-informed direction relax. It is **not** the leader of desire and chemistry. Hips are. Hearts are.

One last note on feminine relaxation: the jaw correlates to the pelvis. Tension in a jaw, equates to tension in a pelvis. I once had a client who, after a horrific accident in which her jaw was broken, stopped feeling any sexual desire. It was as though someone had turned a tap off within her. No desire. No spark. Sexuality on pause. A broken jaw will be reflected in a "locked down" pelvis, tension in the pelvis that prevents the flow of blood and energy. Always include your jaw, neck and shoulders in any feminine embodiment practice you choose.

Amplification

You are a being of amplification. Just like a musical instrument, you can receive a vibration (energy) and make it wider, bigger and felt with more emotion (amplification).

If a guitar were strings only, it would not sound as it does and we would not feel it as we do. It would not be as compelling. A guitar has a body designed to reverberate, to amplify sound and send it out as blissful waves capable of "hitting" people's heart strings and influencing how they feel.

Your body is like the body of a guitar. Strings are like feelings.

As someone plucks the string, it vibrates sound (energy) into the body-space. The body of a guitar is perfectly designed to bounce sound around it, to amplify its vibration and send out notes that can be felt by others.

You, flower, play music just like a guitar. You open to receive energy, just as the strings of a guitar do. You are perfectly designed to receive energy inwards and to *move* in *response* to it, sending it back out into the world as something infinitely more powerful than it was when it first entered you.

You are a being of amplification. You are the amp of life.

Every time you amplify (make it feel even better/turning "the dial" up), you discover you are a sensual genius. Go explore it. The more you feel, the more energy is flowing through you and from you, the more the universe and everything you desire is drawn towards you – including your man and the type of attention you crave. The more you flow, the more ecstatic, vital and magnetic you become.

Amplification: movement

Adding movement (responsiveness) and sound *amplifies* feeling. Energy. E-motion. Be in motion with it. Don't get still! Don't keep a lid on it. Don't throw it out onto someone else. Be with *this* level of energetic abundance in your body, *for* you. This energy is moving through you, *for you*. Move *with* it. What movement do you need to "be with it?" To express it? To let it channel *through* you?

Feel it so fully it dissolves. Emotions only stay stuck in our body, on repeat cycles, when we scratch the record and don't let the full expression move through us. These emotions will keep "hitting play" in our lives, trying to complete their cycles. To heal, we must fully feel, to be able to fully let it go.

> *My son was having a meltdown the other day (30 minutes and I held the WHOLE thing, not even sure how) anyway, at one point I jumped up and down on the spot and shook my body as I could feel myself elevating into my head. Worked perfectly, will keep trying this.*
>
> – Ange

Ask yourself:
What is asking to come through me right now?
When you connect to one part of your body, what movement would have it smiling with a "yes, just like that?"

> *I can't believe how much more I am moving my body; as in rolling my shoulders, shaking my hands and arms, rolling my neck, getting up and rotating my hips when I am feeling stuck, stressed, overwhelmed etc. I used to just stay as still as possible. This feels much better.*
>
> – Ange

Amplification: sound

Women are so afraid of their sound. So conditioned out of our own voice and truth, we are scared to use it. Using sound is perhaps the most radical act of feminine reclaiming. Soften your throat. Relax your neck muscles. Loosen any attachment you have to "polite noises." See what's there.

I learnt how to explore with adding the sound of my body during sex. Not keeping sound "pretty" but really exploring the sounds of deep sensation and pleasure. It's often more of a growl and it feels incredible.

> – Pamela

When something feels good, let the sound of that out! From a hip shake, to a hug, to a beautiful day. What sound does your body make when it takes that beauty or sensation internally? Let that sound out!

Remember, the masculine responds to energy; we're working on getting in greater and greater energetic alignment and truth, not muddying it and soothing it down or closing it up.

When it feels good, I really let myself know it does. When he hugs me, I let out an audible sigh. When he's getting it right I let him know with sound – and he responds by giving me more of that!

> – Rachel

When you connect to a part of your body, what sound would best express the feeling within this part of your body? Can you share it with others outside of you and in doing so, feel it deeper?

I use vocal toning to clear frustration and release stagnant energy, breathwork for shifting emotions and regulating my nervous system. Dance, yoga and wiggling when feeling blocked, flat and reclusive. Especially when mine or my children's nervous system is dysregulated.

> – Allyce

Amplification: Touch

Touch reconnects us to our body. Touch all the soft places on your body (neck, breasts, belly). Use touch to bring you back into your body or help to keep you there. Let go of tension. Relax these areas. There is nothing more ecstatic than watching a woman so completely relaxed in her body as she experiences feeling moving through it and unconsciously moves in response to it. It is the very definition of desire.

> *When we are in a hard conversation, more and more I am realising when I'm getting stiller and stiller, and now I intentionally turn my body towards him, stroke/rub my chest/heart and sometimes rock to try and get back in my body.*
>
> – Ange

Touch and move your body for the sole purpose of feeling *more* and in doing so elicit more energy from it. Embodied movement (responding to body sensation) is not choreographed. It does not originate from the mind. In fact, it's usually pretty ungraceful! But it *will* feel amazing.

Numbness and pain are experiences of the body. Instead of avoiding these sensations, begin to 'enter them' with touch. Touch the places in your body you 'feel nothing' or 'feel too much'. Go gently. Be deeply self compassionate (see numbness and pain).

What do you need to stay here?
What can you give yourself that you've never received?

What is fully listened to is free to be fully dissolved. Pain and numbness can be a pathway to pleasure. When they are fully released from the body, sensitivity floods back in and pleasure arises.

If you find it frustrating or irritating to be with, can you breathe deeply and turn your frustration into fascination?

Can you train your brain to get curious instead of stuck?

When touching these areas, breathe deeply and try asking your intuition "Why is this here? What message do you have for me?" You may feel a little foolish at first, but if you're willing to be patient and loving with your body, you *will* reconnect your inner voice and begin hearing your deep "knowings" once again. Don't rush and put expectations on your body to perform. Be patient, receive anything that arises with gratitude, knowing you are building a muscle that one day will be an incredible asset and the foundation of ecstasy in your body and life.

Amplification is NOT performance

Amplification is **not** performance. You **do not** fake amplifying. You do not amplify for *others*. You amplify to **reclaim**. You amplify to **feel** *more*. You stay connected to *you*, and you ask, *what is here to be felt? What next?* Amplification is an embodiment practice.

Embodiment: to consciously connect to your body with the purpose of eliciting more energy. Embodiment pulls energy *in,* enlivens cells, awakens power. Embodiment asks, *what do I need to feel this even more? To feel even better?*

Performance: doing something with the purpose of being pleasing to the other. Performance leaks energy outwards, is focused on someone or something outside of self. Performance asks, *what do* they *need from me?* It makes assumptions *for* the other person and coerces the self into giving it.

Amplification: the practice of plucking a string of feeling and then discovering how deep and wide you can take that sound and what scales you can play within it. It is an experience of your own pleasure, body and power. It just so happens that when you let energy flow *through* you in *deeper, wider* and more *powerful* ways, mountains pay attention.

Adornment is worship

You were born of, and for, the Goddess, She, Shakti (feminine half of God in Sanskrit). But do you remember you *are* a form of the Goddess, made in her image? That this body of yours *is* the temple of the Goddess? The place of worship? God is not outside of you; She's inside of you.

Your beauty is a gift of the divine, of She.
Yes, *your* beauty.
You are made of curves, valleys and flowing ripples, just as She is.

Every time you acknowledge, appreciate or revel in beauty, you are in Goddess worship.
To deny *your* beauty is to deny *Her,* and isn't the patriarchy doing a good enough job of that already?

[I'm working on] matching my outer with how I'm feeling inside more consciously. So consciously adorning myself – skin care, make-up, earrings, different head bands, wearing dresses, skirts. I love wearing skirts and never really realised how much. My husband likes it too. Not saving the skirts and dresses for "good" or special occasions. It's changed how I feel on a daily basis. Rather than track pants and mum bun (still do this but it's not all the time). Feel so much sexier and as a result we have more sex!

I now have lip glosses everywhere and I'm always putting it on! I feel more plump and luscious rather than dry and dehydrated.

> – Shelley

Since the beginning of time, humans have known this sacred truth: beauty is Her gift. It increases Her energy and power. It's why statues of the Goddess are lovingly covered in gold, strung with flower leis, draped with luxurious cloth, offered sensual delights: food, candles, incense. Anything that amplifies Her beauty, *is* grace.

In a culture that subscribes to an external and limited expression of beauty, that pretends an inner light doesn't exist, that says you need a man or an establishment to access it, adornment is a radial act of honouring. A lost art form of the feminine.

Your body is a temple. Pray, and you will learn how to worship.

You pray when you rub her with oils, creams and loving strokes that cause your heart to bloom.
You pray when you feel her strength and vitality in her movement: dance, yoga, playing.
You pray when you amplify Her delight in her own beauty.

When we adorn our body with cloth that makes us bloom, sculpt our eyes with shades that make us glow, colour our lips with the invitation of *our* pleasure, dangle gold threads around our neck and ears, dazzle and shine our fingers and toes, our energy *amplifies* with each addition. Our light brightens, our energy increases until it is palpable; you are felt before you are seen. When you are seen, you are instantly received as a blessing. This is magnetism.

When practicing the feminine art of adornment, each "addition" gets to feel delightful to you! If it dulls (closes you) instead of shines you (blooms you), it should not be on your temple ... or in your wardrobe! Each piece you select to adorn your temple should free up more energy within you and *amplify* how you feel. You get to feel glorious! Now, as you are. Not when. Not if. Now.

> *I've only discovered how dresses make me feel in the last few years. I love my boho dresses and feel so feminine and full of love. Growing up I was made to feel like I had no right to be or feel special or beautiful. I had to be average and anytime I "stood out" it was squashed by my dad – because how dare I make a scene.*
>
> – Brooke

Adornment is an art that requires cultivation. There are no "fashion rules." Only what feels like a true expression and amplification of who you are and how you feel on the inside – which will change day to day! It's not about staying the "same" or maintaining a daily regime. It is about creating the time to "check in" with yourself before you dress and asking yourself, *what would delight me today?*

Time will not "happen upon you." When seeking change, it is important to "schedule it in" before it becomes a natural way of being for you.

Avoiding creating time to "check in" with yourself can be a self-sabotaging manoeuvre to minimise who you are and how you show up. It can be an avoidance of your power.

There are NO unattractive women. True beauty is infinite. Learnt beauty has a small spectrum and a whole lot of rules as dictated by time, culture and patriarchy. Your light, your energy, your expression, were chosen in this lifetime to bless this earth. To suppress its blessing is a great tragedy. Possibly the greatest.

Open your petals, beauty.
Don't throw your beauty back in the face of the divine.
Don't hurt your body.
Don't hurt your heart.
Don't hurt your soul.
Adorn.

Worship.
Claim your power. Claim the love the divine has for itself in you.

Masculine

*Unsure what the masculine is
in you and your partner ...*

Mountain (masculine energy)

The mountain is the representation of masculine energy in this book. The masculine is consciousness. It's the part of us that always was and always will be. Some of us may identify this aspect of our self as soul.

The masculine within all of us has strengths we shall call "gifts" or "traits." These are the gifts of logic, vision, purpose, structure, leadership, problem solving and goal achievement. In this book, masculine energy is called a mountain because it literally has the presence of a great mountain and more metaphorically because this energy can "move mountains" in pursuit of a goal. This is the energy of hustle. Win, lose. Succeed, fail.

While the masculine within all of us has drive and always seeks the "next goal," it does so because there is an internal desire to one day "be done" and to experience the bliss of "nothingness" (total rest with no demand) – the ultimate freedom. Freedom from mind, constriction and need. Masculine energy hustles for freedom.

The masculine craves to "empty" (the flower craves to fill), to experience nothingness, space, blank walls, blank space, clean, clear, empty space, empty shelves, less is more, aloneness, isolation, quiet – the opposite of the flower.

You might recognise a craving for this same state when you've been in a masculine mind for too long and yell, "Just give me nothing! No kids. No noise. No colour. No light. Just nothing." Heaven ...

Or perhaps you've meditated until you're no longer aware of your body. You're not feeling. You're in a bliss state of "nothing."

"Emptiness" is pure bliss for the mountain.
Nothing. No "content."
No distractions. No disruptions.
Just mind and consciousness.
Bliss.

Penetrate or withdraw

Masculine energy **penetrates** (goes and gets) or **withdraws** (leaves). Feminine energy **opens** (blooms energy out) and **closes** (seals energy up).

A masculine energy sees in black and white, normal or broken; doesn't need attention or needs to be fixed. A feminine energy sees every other possibility and every shade of grey *and* colour.

When tension rises in a mountain and he feels unskilled and unable to "fix what is broken" in front of him, he will seek release from his perceived constraint (lack of freedom) and withdraw (into freedom) in one way or another.

When tension rises in a flower and she feels unmet and unable to fully open and express, she will close up and take her energy back inward.

Withdrawal: Leaving. Ejaculating. "Disappearing" into work, a hobby, the couch or a beer. He may enter depression. He will likely avoid marriage and commitment. He will seek freedom because he *cannot or does not know how* to find it here *with* you.

Penetration: The energy that "pushes." Drives forwards. Focuses on "getting" or achieving a goal. Focus is on self, not other – "what *I* need," "what *I* want," "what *I* think is important."

In general, men withdraw too soon and women close too soon. When either of you closes or withdraws too soon, there is no longer an opportunity for this interaction to get any better.

"Women are too hard," he'll say. "I can't ever get it right"; "I don't know what you need or want!" He'll give up trying. If he can't fix you rationally and he has no other skills, if he stops at his own feeling state, he'll "leave" in one form or another.

The moment you realise any emotion is "just energy" wishing to be expressed through you, and you "kit him up" to roll with holding the space for you without anxiety, fear or pressure to "fix" anything – both of you are going to feel a whole lot better! He'll feel capable of penetrating you, your heart and your energy, and you'll feel safe to open and let him in (receive).

However, depending on the stories and attachments you each have to different emotions, this can be more challenging than you think (revisit the sections dealing with emotion attachment and family patterns).

His withdrawal is an *attempt* at the "reset" phase of the testosterone cycle. Testosterone is on a "build and spend cycle":

- Mission (spending energy/testosterone)
- Conquer (release from constraint, freedom)
- Rest (build and replenish energy/testosterone stores)

The cycle repeats continuously because he's always on mission, isn't he?

What would it look like to consider this as a necessary aspect of his masculine, mountain nature? Just as a flower flows with all the currents, a mountain builds, spends and rests. What if the conversation could be less "be more like me," and more "let's do this, loving our differences"? What would change?

Withdrawal and disappearing should serve his purpose of becoming a better man. His resting phase or activity should be a space where he discovers more of himself, so he can bring more back to his woman and world.

You will know if your man is engaging in unhelpful resting activities because they will not "bring him back better." These "activities" do *not* grow him, but act as a type of bypass of his growth. A way to maintain distance from his woman, intimacy and responsibility.

True spaces of masculine growth involve being completely alone (relying totally on self, discovering more of self) or around other men (who help him rise, call out deficient behaviour and challenge him). You will know these activities because he will return "better," with an enhanced capacity to provide: loving you better, loving your family better, pursing his next goal with increased fervour or impeccability.

Single focus

All of us can identify with this desire for single focus when we're in our masculine energy. You know the feeling, don't you? You've seen your end goal, and all you want is for everyone to leave you alone so you can complete the task unimpeded. It's infuriating when you're interrupted and prevented from finishing, isn't it? I know it feels rageful in my body! But then, I have a well-cultivated masculine, so goals and direction are largely a more comfortable energy for me than feminine magnetism (which I've learnt the skill of and can apply extremely well!).

The mountain state within us all continually focuses on the next goal and attaches freedom to its achievement. Hence, the mountain will be forever seeking freedom from constraint – perceived or real.

The completion of *this* task will give him freedom.
If he finally reached *that* spot on the corporate ladder, he'd experience freedom.
When he has *the* watch, accomplishment, accolade, orgasm ... he'll finally feel free ...

If you are the flower within your relationship, you will be able to see single focus drive more frequently in your partner. What you will notice is how he is *always* "on mission," always in pursuit of his next goal.

> *I'm going to teach a class while my husband lays sod with one of our sons. Iced matcha latte in my hand that he brought home for me. We've been working on this yard for five days! Five days of parenting, practice, and watching this man provide the design I created for our home. Celebrating this win. Celebrating him rising to all the challenges. We even spoke about his dad, who would take him off task (sorting all his sports cards) and make him farm, giving him a hard time that farming is more important. His way or the highway sort of thing.*
>
> *This really inspired me not only seeing the value in and respecting his single focus, but to see my sons' values and missions. I feel I've practised this, encouraging them in what they value, but to see just how important seeing and hearing them is. This beautiful yard will be a constant reminder to soften and trust his masculine.*
>
> – Hannah

Masculine energy is the force of provision within all of us. This energy seeks to be of service and to provide freedom, continually. He will use the skills he already has to provide and develop them as he does; this is part of "building" a strong mountain. Sometimes this provision will be emotional, sometimes physical, sometimes practical. The form of the provision is not relevant; it only matters that the provision exists. As he "grows" in provision capability, his ability to gift freedom extends beyond himself and into wider and wider circles: woman, family, community.

Whether *you* think it's a worthy goal/task or not is not up for discussion here. I first want you to see how he *is* the knight in shining armour, the hero on a quest. All. The. Time. He is always seeking to provide. You just may never have noticed it before.

> *I love it when I can see the purpose and outcome later. But never at the time lol. For example a few weekends ago he spent half the day so focused on pulling apart one of my boys' darn iPads! He had no time for me or anyone else. Hardly spoke to me. I felt rejected as I was in a real lovey-dovey social mood. He was not. It was only later when my son was so happy to have his school iPad fixed that I realised he had saved us hundreds of dollars! Then I could see the benefit and "love" his single focus.*
>
> – Nicole

He needs challenge to rise stronger and build a "better" mountain. Estimable acts build self-esteem. The sensation of completing his quest builds his sense of self-worth and confidence in his ability to provide. A mountain grows the more he can trust himself to do hard things, to complete and provide in the face of challenge.

Truly, whether his provision is noticed or not, he is there, quietly working away at what he perceives (with the information he has at this time in your relationship) will provide you, him and your family a better life. Of course, it is the same for you in your masculine energy.

> *In every minute of his spare time my hubby is working on his trailer and perfecting its setup ... He could spend the whole day there if he was able! I'm often with our daughter thinking "ugh why doesn't he come and spend time with us instead of tinkering away by himself over there."*
>
> *So today when he started sharing about getting close to finishing this trailer I thought of today's single focus and cycle of completion chat and I asked him "ok, so when you finish the work you want to do on the trailer, what will it provide you?"*
>
> *His eyes lit up, and he spoke so animatedly for a good five minutes listing all the ease, space, and FREEDOM it would bring to all areas of his life and work day especially so that – you guessed it – he could come home and spend more full presence with us.*
>
> – Allyce

Beginning to see differently

When you nail this, it is literally life changing. Your heart blooms towards your partner in appreciation and your relationship dynamic changes instantly and forever.

In the eyes of appreciation, we are no longer asking our lover to change or to be different. We love them just as they are, and that is all any human ever wants. The paradox is, the moment you love someone as they are, they are free to change, and likely will. The light that would otherwise be so busy projecting *out*, defending and defensively reflecting against "a threat," turns inwards. It shines on what we ourselves wish to change, for *us*. It is here change becomes *possible*. *Not* when our message is, you are **not** okay as you are.

For many years I have wished for a beautiful veggie garden (many so-so or half-hearted attempts). But since starting your programs things have changed and hubby is so onboard, he is majestic. He has made plans, sourced materials, arranged deliveries and seen the first phase of OUR project to completion. Which is so mind blowingly sexy in its masculinity and resulted in some super steaminess and earthmoving new discoveries.

And one other beautiful and amazing thing was we worked together as partners, companionably, supportively and lovingly (big change) to consciously create this for our family and to make memories of each other. Seeing him single focused was wonderful to behold. This work has such ripples both in and outside the bedroom.

– Candee

He's always "on mission." The more you train yourself to see it, the more appreciation builds, the more room there is for change.

If you can't see his provision or you don't understand what his chosen task is serving, ask him!

Honey, what do you see … (the thing he's doing) … as providing?

Be willing to listen, with curiosity and an open heart, mind and body: "What is here I've never seen before? What can I learn about my partner?"

> *I've also noticed through observing that I really have NO FREAKING CLUE what the hell is going on most of the time!?!?! I'm like "is it this? is it this? Remember this is not about you" and so I watch him and ask him questions and when he answers, it's always with something that hadn't even crossed my mind for second! So funny.*
>
> – Allyce

This is the time to practise your art of receiving:
Receive all the ways in *his* mind, however misguided, he *believes* he's providing for you or your family.
Receive his intention as the energy you've been *craving* from him.
Let yourself feel this moment of love so completely it melts your heart open.

Let's practise what this change in perception looks like.

He may be polishing his car:
Old you: *What an a-hole. The kids are screaming, climbing all over me, and he's out there shining his car. I never do that. He doesn't even consider me.*

New you: *Oh! He's shining his car so we can take a Sunday drive together. He sees his car as honouring to the beauty he wishes to create for me and our family.*

He may be chopping watermelon when the kids are screaming, a glass just broke and the baby needs a nappy change:

Old you: *Far out! It's always me! If I wasn't here, this would fall to shit! I always have to tell him what to do, he's hopeless. He has NO idea. Can't he SEE the chaos? He doesn't care enough about me to help. He takes me for granted. I'm the servant.*

New you: *Ah. I asked him to make a snack for the kids who were hungry. He believes if he completes this snack the kids will calm down, which will help me. He's doing what I asked, which he thinks is what I want, providing for me and his kids.*

Practise seeing with a new lens. If you can't see, ask! He'd love to share his dreams and desire with you, I'm sure.

> *He has been in the garage ALL day. Previously this was unheard of. And would annoy the crap out of me. Not anymore because ...*
>
> *1. Look at him. Actually fixing something. Super-focused. Using those IT office job hands. Super sexy.*
>
> *2. This shows me if he can do this and be so dedicated to his car, then it really can be anything! Like our house, which is in desperate need of renovating and fixing!*
>
> *3. And lastly ... This has given me a great opportunity today to let him be, do his thing. No judgement, no bitchy remarks and instead ... Praise the shit out of him, love him hard, and tell him how sexy this is.*
>
> *So much polarising in our home today. Me inside dancing. Being.*

Loving on kids visiting friends. And him super-focused, and in his zone. Super delicious.

Thank you Julie for opening me up to different perspectives but mostly to him. This masculine man who is before me. Who I've never seen and who is now RISING as I rise in my feminine.

– Nicole

When your interruption from his single focus does not feel good

Think about the times you've been focused on a time-pressured task, or just one you *really* want to complete because it will feel so good (freedom for self) or provide something wonderful for your home/company/family (freedom for others).

Can you tap in to how that building drive to complete feels in your body and mind? Can you tap in to how annoying it is, if not infuriating, when you're interrupted by someone who needs something *else* from you (child/colleague/partner)? Can you see your vision, desire and goal slipping further and further away? How do you feel? Strong or irritated, defeated and unvalued?

It is the same for all of us in our masculine, but it is more frequent for the partner who holds the most masculine energy. The greater the masculine energy, the greater the frequency and strength of the masculine traits. Again, this is not to judge but to empower your relationship. Imagine how this would change your experience of love, connection and communication if this were "just a known fact" and you both knew how to communicate in these phases!

Before you interrupt a single focus mission, first stretch to see if his provision is an act *for* you. Ask yourself in this moment, *what are the possible benefits to me, to our family, to the things I treasure most in this lifetime, of him doing this? How is this ON the way to what I love and value too?*

> *Once upon a time I would have thought his disengagement was disinterest in ME, not caring, not listening but now when I see and feel it, it pulls me back into gratitude for his service of me and his single focus as a huge dedication of love for me and our family.*
>
> – Sarah

If you can see how he's trying to provide *for* you, it will dramatically change what happens in the moments that follow and in your relationship long-term.

Possible reactions you'll notice from your mountain (or they'll notice from you!) being interrupted during a single focus mission:

- Agitation, irritation or frustration in his voice or actions
- Distracted responses, abrupt quality to interactions
- Frowning, huffing, fidgety
- Interrupting your share or request
- A desire to fix and provide solutions, not to sit in emotions
- Little engagement to what is actually being said, one-word replies
- A sense of "tapping his toes," a desire to get the conversation done as quickly as possible
- Eye rolls, "here we go again" attitude
- Withdrawal – emotionally or physically, no reply

> *Previously, as soon as I felt something I would go to him and feel that intense "need" to share – and if I saw him doing something that I didn't recognise as important (as it wasn't one of my values)*

I would just steamroll in and start sharing. He would try to finish the conversation as quickly as possible by bringing in solutions and fixes, he would often get agitated and snap at my feelings, he would interrupt, shift his weight between his feet, physically wanting to run from the space etc.

– Cindy

When you know this is just part of being in your masculine, you get to decide what needs to change to create greater relationship harmony. You'll both cycle here, but remember, it will be more frequent for the more masculine partner.

For instance, when I'm in "work mode," I'm fully in my masculine. Go, go, go, no breaks. I know that if I'm allowed the space and time to fully immerse and can *use* all of this intense energy, I can move mountains and shift a week's worth of work in an hour. But if I'm interrupted, it takes *more* time to get back into that intense energy-flow and longer *still* to pick up where I'd left off. My productivity reduces; my frustration and tension increase. My love-flow is near non-existent because I'm not focused on my body, heart or relationships. I'm in the land of the mind, logic and consciousness.

It is this understanding that has allowed me to be a full-time stay-at-home mum to four children *and* have two very successful businesses. When I'm in my masculine flow, both my husband and I "protect that space" because when I exit it, having achieved and completed my missions, I'm a much better lover and mother, now free to fully immerse back in my feminine.

The thing is, I also respect this drive and need in my husband. It goes both ways, but it begins with acknowledging its existence and importance.

Respectful single-focus shifts that have had enormous impact on relationship connection:

> *We have actually agreed the morning isn't a time for any discussion requiring anything I want/need his focus on. If it's REALLY important he calls back later in the morning. He's had to learn not to just walk out and I had to learn to hold the tension in my body and be ok with the "time to talk" not being on my time line.*
>
> – Cindy

> *We agreed to not bring anything up while he was getting ready for work, and with the framework now of "I'd love to talk to you about 'x'; when would be a good time for you?" It's really made a big difference! Also understanding his values and looking for that single focus on his task and respecting that. It has meant when I do have his presence I have it FULLY and he is less likely to collapse into frustration and snap back while I'm full feeling. Also he tries to fix less when I'm not interrupting him.*
>
> – Allyce

When your interruption from his single focus feels good

The concept that feminine energy is in and of itself a blessing is one of the ideas women struggle with the most. No less and no more than a blessing of consciousness or having a prayer laid upon you, but a blessing that involves energy.

If you have muddled conceptions around what the feminine is and is not (especially if you attach this energy to women only), this can be a hard pill to swallow. I'd love to think it's the easiest one for you, but I've found it is not. Women who define themselves by masculine measures struggle enormously to contemplate the influence their energy has and the ability that they have to reclaim exceptional rejuvenation and healing within any relationship or space.

Interestingly, men don't struggle with this concept at all. They understand it the instant you mention it. Mountains are fully aware of the power of flower (feminine) energy.

The feminine can bless a space with her energy at 5% or at 100% and you *will* feel the difference. A feminine being in a feminine body that has learnt how to open to receive energy and how to let it flow in undulating ripples through her body blesses each of us. It is this transmission of energy, when sent through a being of amplification, that can break our heart, make us weep, open our body to desire and ecstasy and make us remember life. The good stuff. The stuff we're here for, the reason we're "in this" to begin with.

> *His absolute favourite thing to do is watch me move. Clothed, not clothed, washing dishes … doesn't matter. It fuels him. Me moving through the house is art to him.*
>
> – Carlie

In your truest self, you as a feminine incarnation are a blessing the moment we witness you and feel your energy.

> *He especially loves when I arrive somewhere after him and enter the space. He gloats and always says he thinks "that's my wife," a sense of pride and loving ownership.*
>
> – Sharon

It is this feminine energy "transmission" that is life-giving for any of us in our masculine, where we are more consciousness and less energy. When we receive this feminine blessing, the masculine within each of us relaxes; tension drains from our body. We feel renewed and ready to get back on task with reignited energy. The feminine is life-giving energy.

This is why the masculine within all of us, and most especially among those of us who animate more masculine energy, continually "seeks out" ripples of feminine energy because instinctively, like a survival hardwiring, we know it is this energy that complements our purpose, allows us to *be* manifest and have a force in the world at all.

Here's what some of my client's partners have to say about this:

> *It makes me feel close to you.*
>
> – Andrew

> *It makes me feel loved and special … lights that fire in my belly. The compassion that you have for me fills my cup.*
>
> – Ben

For instance, in the example from the previous section, where I'm in my full masculine force, my husband is equally in his feminine energy. He'll be child-minding, playing, pottering, eating, drinking, laughing etc. He's lightness and energy. I'm denseness and consciousness. In this state, I'm not connected to my body and enjoy being focused on my work (mission) SO much that eating and drinking do not seem important. Without my husband "interrupting" me by nourishing me with food, drinks and his loving touch, I simply wouldn't nourish my body and eventually my energy would collapse, my body now run into the ground and both of us completely disconnected.

His feminine energy coming towards my masculine energy to feed me, with the sole purpose of "looking after me" and nourishing me so I can perform at my peak, is a blessing I am always incredibly grateful for and feel rejuvenated by. His "loving touch" when I'm not connected (on mission) reminds me of love, life and my energy. His presence and attention in his feminine brings my attention down from my head and into my body and heart. I feel loved. I feel considered and appreciated. I want to be with him more. Only moments previously, I wasn't even aware he existed, so lost in my mission was I. This is the power of the feminine.

When "She's" *in* on your mission, when she wants you to succeed, she's every angel, enchantress and auspicious charm that has ever helped the weary hero on his quest.

> *My fiancé told me tonight, "At one point today when you walked in the room it was like a breath of fresh air, a nice break from my uni assignment. I like the lightness you have about you."*
>
> *I was bewildered that he sensed my feminine, so I asked, "That surprises me. Did we embrace? Did you stop to interact with me?"*
>
> *He said, "No, it just felt nice. Whenever I feel a bit sick of a task I often come look for you and ask how you are going."*
>
> *Me, still bewildered beyond belief that he is actually seeking me, the magnet, out for rejuvenation.*
>
> – Megan

Of course, I offer this same energetic "gifting" back to my husband when our energies are reversed. This is simply the understanding that the masculine within all of us *needs* nourishing and the feminine within all of us *is* deeply nourishing.

When we flow in our feminine, our natural feminine gifts flow effortlessly. When we're in our masculine trying to deliver feminine gifts, it's hard work and likely you'll resent them.

The 30 second pause

If you ask your mountain a question or a thought to ponder, that too becomes a single focus. For a flower who has 50 tabs open in "the browser of her mind" at any given time, this feels ridiculous and infuriating, but the mountain only ever has **one**.

Remember, the more masculine, the more "empty." The more feminine, the more "full." This is reflective of these different communication abilities.

For a mountain animating a lot of masculine energy to answer you thoroughly (remember the masculine brain thinks in success or fail, do or do not), he has to:

- Close the single-focus browser he has open in his mind
- Shutdown the search engine.
- Relaunch the search engine, maybe even update it
- Single-finger type his question in the search engine of his mind
- Browse all the suggested answers, possibilities and logical considerations
- Click the link he thinks is the best match
- Read the blog, decide if it's the answer he needs
- If yes, great. He's ready to share his findings with you.
- If no, then he begins the process again

It takes an inordinate amount of time. Truly. Avoid blaming, judging or criticising. This is one of the main differences between a masculine mind and a feminine mind, and there are benefits and drawbacks to each way of being, so don't assume one is better than the other. Learn to work with it instead of fighting it.

> *As he spoke I listened … And each time I counted to 30 he then went on to speak for another few minutes with even more excitement to share! In my mind I was thinking WOW you've got so much to say on this and I had no idea! So great.*
>
> – Allyce

Each time you ask a question or for feedback, wait 30 seconds. Literally count to 30 in your mind. If he still hasn't answered, count to 30 again, and again … until he does finally respond. If you jump in too soon you'll miss the best parts of what he thinks or has to say. If you want to be fully met, wait. He will bring you his "fullness" and penetrate you with everything he has when he's given enough time to process and work with his "natural cycles."

> *I remember with the deepest compassion that if I want him to be all the beautiful masculine things, they come with "limitations." Every time I think I've waited long enough, count to 30 and wait again, and again. Imagine him learning to read, be patient, open. Give him time to think and process.*
>
> – Cathy

Be patient. Be the sun. Wait for him to find his inner compass and orient towards you. And, as with everything in this book, this can be reversed if *you* are the one animating masculine energy.

Working with the mountain's single focus

Knowing what you now know about the masculine and its single focus drive, you may find yourself wondering "does this mean I can't interrupt him?" The answer is this: you can, but do it artfully and you will receive an artful response. Do it disrespectfully and full of your own inner irritation and discomfort, and *that* is the quality of response you will get back. You go first; the universe responds.

The way to approach mountain energy in single focus and be met with full presence involves four steps:

1. Observe and get clear; ask yourself "What is he in provision of here? What is his mission? What does that mission's completion seek to be in service to?"

2. If you are unsure, ASK HIM! **With** curiosity. "What can't I see here? Can you show me?" Don't move on from here until you are clear on his mission, not your predilections.

Add in an adaptation from Alison Armstrong's *The Queen's Code*:

3. To put a desire of yours on his goals:
   • Be in your feminine invitation energy (revisit the "Feminine" section)
   • Touch him (bring presence into his body)
   • Wait for him to orient towards you
   • Ask for a time that he can show up for you (and you become the single focus), roughly how long it should take, and what it's in relation to

   E.g. "Honey, I would love to sit together and talk about ... it should only take … when would work for you to discuss this?"

Or, more simply: "Babe, I'd love to talk about … it should only take … when works for you?"

This alleviates any anxiety of "oh no, here we go again, what have I done this time …" It respects his need to complete task-cycles. It allows his brain time to compartmentalise, ruminate on "the thing" and arrive prepared with full focus.

It respects *you* because you're saying **you're worthy** of 100% presence and attention, not a diluted percentage.

You do need a time he commits to coming back to you and follows through on. Accountability and self-discipline are core building blocks of the mountain. It can be in an hour or two, tomorrow night or a week from now, depending on how much "thinking" or emotional processing time he requires in relation to the topic, but you do need a set time and date for his accountability and your nervous system relaxation.

4. After the discussion, when what each of you want is clear, the last question before wrapping up is "what might the other need to be able to provide that 'thing' for you?" Of course, this is a question you can each take it in turns of asking the other, but for this scenario we will focus on one person.

    We are not in this relationship to "get"; we're in this relationship to "give" love and "receive" a better quality of love in return. When we feel supported by our partner, when we feel we're on the same team and have each other's backs, it removes the fear of pass or fail and we are naturally inclined to provide a better quality of love and care. This question lays this foundation.

What do you need to be able to provide this?

If it's an in-depth or difficult conversation, you can use this sentence when setting up your "discussion date" time *and* you can use it when working out how to implement the desired change.

In the set-up scenario, you're asking to see if he needs anything from you or that can be provided (child-free time, a time he's not tired, additional information ...) in order for him to feel able to be there, at that time, with that conversation.

In the ending scenario, you're asking what he might need from you to be able to provide everything you're desiring. What does *he* need to be able to put in place for the changes you desire?

He may need nothing! Often he doesn't, but it is an important question for respectful communication.

Of course, this framework can be used by either partner at any time.

What single focus can feel like for a flower witnessing it

Single focus feels like a building fury for the feminine. There's an intensity and a density that goes along with the masculine's single focus that flowers often struggle with. So let's lay it out here.

You're more sensitive to the flow of love energy between you; it is your natural gift. You will likely register the shift in his energy density before he's even aware of it.

When he's on mission and all his conscious energy is directed towards solving a problem or completing a task and his reward is freedom, there's an intensity to his focus that blocks out all else. To the flower, this can feel like an angry storm; she can feel the energy get dense and "brew" within him. As a girl conditioned to "being nice" and feeling connection, you may read this as "he's mad with me." Though your body may register this density of energy as "anger," there *genuinely* is nothing wrong. *You've* done nothing wrong. This is the energy he needs to muster to complete his "mission." He's not mad at you. **He's just focused** on moving mountains.

> *Holy shivers. We're packing up our caravan and I feel like he's mad at me, but he's not. He's just very very focused on completing a big task.*
>
> *I always feel like he's mad at me while he's doing this kind of stuff. But he's not. He's just a very single focused masculine being and he's not paying me attention.*
>
> *When he's done he'll come and slap me on the toosh and give me a smooch, and now I get why. This is revolutionary.*
>
> > – Carlie

When in the face of this fury, flowers tend to split into two distinct categories:

- The ones who seek to soothe him, making it easier on him, worried they've put too much on him and backtrack
- The ones who seek to take over and rise to the challenge

instead of him

Flower, instead of trying to save him from challenge or *be* the mountain *instead* of him, sit back. Step into your feminine energy of relaxing into letting that which you desire come towards you. Receive. Relax on your roots, and **find a way** to **enjoy** watching *him* grow. Find a place within you that *knows* this challenge is **beautiful** for him.

Imagine you're the princess (or queen if you prefer!) at a medieval jousting tournament. Sit in the stalls (sit back and observe him). Find the place within you that is enamoured by his skill and provision (beam it out like a Care Bear!), and if a task has been particularly challenging for him to master or complete, acknowledge his victory! Let yourself celebrate it; let him feel it. Let yourself swoon into your champion; let him feel his victory with you. Plant a kiss if you like!

> *When you include touch and closeness in acknowledging my efforts it feels way better! Then it feels like it comes from your heart. It becomes more of "a moment."*
>
> – Nick (my husband)

Begin to pay attention to this single-focus intensity. Instead of crumpling in his presence and attaching meaning (assuming), sit back as a princess in a medieval tournament and enjoy his effort, or ask him for clarity.

The perfect experience of this single focus intensity for me was my "chicken coop story."

After working all Saturday morning I walked into the kitchen and said "hello" to my lover with a kiss, while he was making lunch for us. But something felt off. He seemed deep in thought, distracted from "being here" with me, condensed into his own world.

I watched him for a while trying to put my finger on the funky feeling in my body. *Is he grumpy with me? Is he angry I've left him with the kids all morning?* I asked myself. *Is he in single focus with the roast vegetable focaccia arrangement for lunch …?* I couldn't place it, this funky feeling now pervading my body.

So I asked him, "Hey, you okay?"

"Yeah, fine," he answered, and went back to his focaccia making.

I watched longer, waited. Nope. Funky feeling still in my body. I still felt like he was mad with me. So I asked again, "Are you sure you're okay? Are we okay? You seem angry or grumpy with me or something?"

"No, I'm good, we're good," he replied, and went back to sandwich making.

I stood in the kitchen, perplexed. His words were saying "he's all good," and I've learnt to take him at his word, not read between the lines, but my body was saying "we're *not* good." I just could not put a finger on it! It was an irritating, unsettled dichotomy in my body and my mind. I decided to get close to him and ask again, with more energy and therefore evoking more presence.

"Hey, I'm feeling this really funky disconnection between us in my body," I said. "I hear you saying you're good, but I can't work out why my body feels so off. I feel like you're mad with me. What's going on in your mind at the moment?"

"Well, it's just the chicken coop gate. I can't work out why it's not working …" And on he went with his current challenge, the single focus that he was still on in his mind.

"Oh!" I exclaimed. "That makes sense! Thank you!"

It wasn't that he was annoyed at me working or that he was frustrated by being a solo parent for the morning. He was just single-focused. The guilt, shame and pain this conversation subverted was extraordinary, as has every moment of clarity since. Try it.

Competition and challenge

Have you ever noticed how mountains constantly compare, and often play a jab-and-stab one-upmanship with each other that seems (inexplicably) to *increase* connection between them? For a flower, this feels like death by a thousand cuts. For the mountain, it feels like a reason to shine and polish their mountain-ness.

A mountain cannot know how to be greater or grander without this competitive edge, calling out from him something that would otherwise lie dormant. Competition in its light form asks the other to rise and calls out the warrior to do something he's never done before, to build, refine and perfect what he's capable of, increasing his strength, self-belief and mastery.

The masculine grows through overcoming challenge and surpassing the strength and sense of self he previously held, especially when there is a looming threat of death: conquer against all odds, or die. Both are equal experiences of release and freedom for the mountain.

It's why traditionally masculine rites of passage include isolation, challenge and the threat of certain death. It sharpens his focus, gives him superpowers he previously didn't hold; it builds what he's able to bring back in integrity, honour and service to his family and community.

It is also why he'll choose to invest in "the fight" – be it *in* sport, *watching* sport, game fishing, the war movie, the hero movie, winning the next argument/contest etc. He feels a sense of freedom watching the fight; even if he himself is not directly involved, he finds he disappears into the masculine's favourite place of "nothingness," consumed with the challenge and ultimate attainment of rising or dying, release and freedom.

The masculine needs the experience of challenge to thrive. It is under the experience of rising to a challenge that he builds his sense of self, his ability to provide, and pushes himself to achieve greatness beyond his perceived limits. Without challenge, he'd happily stay in nothing-bliss. Competition and challenge build a mountain, make him stand stronger, command more respect and hold more presence – all of which the flower enjoys immensely and wants for her lover.

It's why I love a strong coach. A strong coach will take you further than you can take yourself. They will challenge your edges and will not seek to solve the problem *for* you or rescue you from the pain of struggle. A strong coach will watch over you, protect the space and ensure you succeed, holding strong their belief that you *will* rise. Such can be true in sport, the armed forces, game fishing or any arena the mountain is called to grow.

Getting comfortable with watching my son struggle has been one of my biggest teachers. I have an innate desire to buffer the "hardness," or save him from the pain, which is a very feminine way of viewing challenge. A flower grows in praise and support; a mountain grows in challenge and competition. I can now see through the lens of a growing mountain, and I can see the beauty in his struggle: the respect, integrity and worth inbuilt in his triumph over challenge. Internally, I now "bow" to his father, coach or friends in deep appreciation when they offer him challenge to rise to. I see the men who hold the space and watch him, but don't save him, and wait ever so patiently for him to rise. Now I use my full feminine force to convey "I believe in you" and celebrate him on his "return" to family and community. Such is a masculine rite of passage.

Feel uncertain whether he can 'handle you'
as you try to open or 'change the game'

Density

The more masculine energy someone animates, the more "dense" and mountain-like their body becomes, built for provision, penetration and drive, not for energy-flow and sensitivity. Think about the ballet dancer vs. the Navy Seal. One is built for flow, movement, feeling and sensitivity. The other for strength, durability and non-emotional decision making.

Of course, there is a spectrum of masculine and feminine energy within all of us. At different times we will *all* feel more sensitive and flowy or more rational and goal-focused. The point of this is not to create a "rule" that says mountains are without feeling and flowers are without rational thinking. We are far more complex than that. It is simply to highlight in the simplest terms the distinct differences between masculine and feminine energy as they exist within ourselves and our partners and influence our relationship. From these understandings, you can extrapolate out to de-code the unique masculine/feminine make-up of both you and your partner.

Mountain are dense, built for consciousness, not for energy-flow. He is not sensitive to the flow of energy and emotions. He lives in the world of the mind, the big picture and the tasks required to complete it. For all of us, in our masculine energy, we can forget we even *have* a body, we're so connected to our mind:

- Forget to eat and drink
- Forego sleep in pursuit of our tasks
- Not realise we have legs until we bring awareness to them
- Not even think about our lover or our children until we're no longer focused on our demanding task

As a flower, this would never happen to you! You're always in touch with how you feel, how your body feels, what your body and feelings need, registering heart-hurts and heart-longings, feeling the people you love. All day, you're tracking your heart and the flow of love. He is not.

He is *not* connected to his heart and feelings while in his masculine. He is connected to his mind, thought and consciousness. Of course, you're the same when animating a large amount of masculine energy!

It's why we *all* need the feminine within us and within relationship. Without this feminine force, we could quite literally run our body into the ground. The feminine within all of us nurtures, nourishes and restores vitality.

It is why when *any* of us are animating a large amount of masculine energy for an extended period of time we will crave the feminine to "feed us," to restore life to our body and love to our heart. In this way we "remember." We "remember" why we're here, the good stuff. We "remember" how we love and who we love. We enjoy all the sensations and vibrancy of life. If we stay in our masculine, there is no vibrancy; it's conscious "nothingness."

We will seek this nourishing feminine energy from people around us, from TV, from a chosen activity that stimulates sensation and feeling, from nature. The feminine revitalises our mind by replenishing our body and energy stores.

The greater the masculine energy within a person, the greater their need for an equally strong feminine replenishment energy. Hence, we end up with jocks and cheerleaders, models and moguls: two equal and opposite energy forces, offering each other the counter-balance they require.

The mountain's density means it takes quite a lot of energy for *anything* to register. It's why the jock and the mogul do not end up with the straight-laced, masculine-energy lawyer; there's not enough energy to register within him. This type of relationship (mogul/lawyer) is a rather bland landscape without the spark of attraction and desire. Of course, they could end up with a passion-filled relationship if one of them is also high-energy flow, but if they're the same, the force of attraction is neutral or repulsive.

He's consciousness. He's not feeling. He doesn't pick up on subtlety because the energy is *too small*. Really. If he can't feel and see your truth in real ways and in real time, he *doesn't know* it exists. He's not being an insensitive, clueless a-hole on purpose. He's just dense. It is his nature.

Before you curse him for "not getting you," take a little moment to practise with your feminine energy: **amplify**! The release of energy will push you back into your feminine polarity, where you will experience release and replenishment and he'll register a response, which gives him something to work with and you something to receive!

No more subtlety. If I am being subtle I realise he won't get it. When I am clear with my feelings and direct but kind with my words, he responds immediately and wants to do anything I need! All I have to do is ask. Which is hard while I get used to it. When you've spent your whole relationship thinking he should "just this" and "just that" and "why can't men just know what we want." Understanding his density has been really important for us. It's like he doesn't have to de-code anymore.

– Keits

Learning how to let him see, hear and feel your truth (not a diluted version)

Think of a flower's responsiveness and a mountain's natural density like ripples in a pond (you may like to revisit the "Masculine" section before you come here). The flower is the water; the mountain is the banks of the pond.

A pebble (disturbance/feeling) is thrown into a still pond. In response to this energy-stimulation (emotion/feeling), the water begins to ripple outwards. From the very centre, in larger and larger waves, the ripples visibly roll upon the pond's surface, until they reach the banks. The disturbance so visible, so tangible, it wakes the banks up.

Now the masculine energy can see, hear and feel the disturbance; he is aware and able to respond.

If, when a pebble drops, the pond swallows it up, keeping her surface completely still, there is *nothing* for the banks to register. Life is "normal." He is blissfully *unaware* there was a disturbance at all.

Anyone holding a strong masculine polarity is not sensitive in the way feminine energy-holders are. A mountain (masculine energy human) can't read below the surface. He's not good at guessing. He's fairly hopeless at "reading between the lines" or anticipating what's below the surface. As are any of us in our masculine.

Without ripples of clear disturbance, there is *nothing* that informs him how to respond. Without ripples, he is singularly focused on whatever his project is at this moment, pursing it unaware of the "environment" or subtle energy.

> *I'm realising I don't feel safe to express and share my energy. I was shut down as a child and as a child it was dangerous. Huge shifts!!! Huge realisations!!!*
>
> – Nicole

If he can't see it, he doesn't know it's there. Men don't know how to be responsive to your truth if they've never seen, heard or felt your truth. Men are either *clueless* because women don't tell them their truth, or *clued-in* when women visibly and authentically respond to their own energy in such a way it is visible to him.

He's responding to your energy and your body. If you flow, he'll respond. If you stay still, there's nothing for him to read, understand or be with.

This doesn't have to be scary, it *can* feel good. It begins always as self-practice. Go back to the section "How to establish your feminine practice" and you will learn *how* to do it. The next part is to be aware of your conditioning that holds you back with falsity and closure. Go back to the section on feminine rejection and get clear on what you're ready to let go and re-write.

Then you're ready for partner-practice. Try it out in small ways, "testing" the waters before you take a huge leap into the deep end. Go as fast as the slowest part of you. This is always the pathway to transformation, not trying to fast-track and shock your system (that's masculine practice).

Slowly and gently.

Learning your energy communication

Women will often use words as weapons or armoury and then double that impact by closing off any feminine energy-flow (he can't read you) and go "straight in" with intense demanding communication or mothering penetrating instructions. This is a masculine communication style.

Direct communication (penetration) may seem the most effective and efficient way to get what you want across but that's a very masculine thought process. Efficiency. Time management. Effectiveness. Productivity. Outcome. Feminine communication is all about how the exchange *feels* and what the flow of energy and love is, not how fast it is resolved.

While is seems rational and clear, it is *not* amplification or clarity of energy-transmission. If you animate your masculine energy in communication with him, he only has two choices:

- Meet *your* masculine with *his* masculine and he'll either penetrate back (fight) or withdraw (dismiss and leave)
- Reflexively drop into his feminine, feel hurt and possibly defensive

Neither of those are a great outcome. If you want a response from your partner that both you and he will enjoy, get in your feminine! The feminine does not communicate from the mind. She communicates from her body and deals specifically in energy and feeling.

Think about your toddler. You don't have to guess what they're feeling, do you? You don't have to wait for them to speak the perfect sentence and clue you in on their thoughts, do you? It's written all over them. No guessing required. You see it, you feel it, and you're motivated to respond to it. There's no hiding and there's no guessing. And the moment you meet them exactly where they are, offer them your calm presence and validate exactly what they're feeling, it shifts, doesn't it? It is the same for flowers learning to feel and reveal.

You do not *tell* him.

Communicate with "I feel" and stay in touch with your body and heart (embodiment and presence).

For example:
Telling: *Can you please fix the gate today?*
Embodied: *I feel nervous that I can't shut the gate on my own (said with truthful feeling)*

Telling: *You need to respond to our child like this.*
Embodied: *I feel scared when you ignore our child (said with truthful feeling), my tummy knots and my heart throbs and I know you love him, but I feel scared … It's so sexy watching you parent with total presence, I feel my heart burst open to you and all I want to do is be around you.*

Telling: *Have you paid the energy bill yet?*

Embodied: *I feel so looked after when you take care of the bills without me having to worry and I feel alone when it feels like my responsibility only.*

Telling: *This isn't doing it for me.*
Embodied: *Hmmmm, I'd really love to feel ...*

Embodied responding is not about saying words. It's about connecting to the truth of the feeling within you and being vulnerable enough to let him see, hear and *feel* it from you. Give him your embodied truth, but then let *him* navigate and decide what to *do* with it.

The solutions he comes up with on his own are worth ten of the solutions you give him. We all know this to be true, right? The lessons you learnt yourself were worth ten of the ones your parents warned you about, weren't they?

Don't *tell* him; lead him and direct him like his mother or boss. *Show* him your feeling and the effect of every moment on your feelings. Talk only about how you *feel*, not what you think. Let the energy you release from your heart, body and emotions do all the talking. A picture's worth a thousand words, right?

> *My responsibility is my clarity of transmission. When I get just a part of what I asked for, instead of getting irritated, I breathe, close my eyes, take a moment and try again. Simplify my language, get clear, reveal my feeling and energy. This has made a huge difference to how I respond to results and disappointment in expectations not being met.*
>
> – Cathy

But how does one become the beacon of such attention and desire if you find yourself in a relationship where he's seemingly more interested in the TV, his beer or his work?

The trick is to step into the energy you were *designed* to pulsate with. The Goddess does not go chasing the mortal male. Can you imagine it? Her, in all her divinity, needing to *chase* and *demand* he pay attention? No. She *becomes* magnetic. She draws *towards* her that which She desires. She *invites*; She does not penetrate to get what She wants.

Like a bee to honey, he *cannot* resist. She becomes the *invitation* he desires to serve and the prize he desires to claim. He wants to be worthy of her. He wants to worship at her altar. But not a single word has been spoken.

Are you feeling challenged at this moment? Want to throw your hands up in exasperation and say "Julie. Seriously. This is a lot of work. Why do I have to do all this? Why can't he just give it to me?"

To which I will say to you this, my darling. You don't have to *do* anything. Ever. If you love being in your masculine and you love attracting a partner in their feminine, then there is nothing for you change! If you adore the chase, the hunt and the hustle in relationship and life, then there's nothing for you to change! But, if you have a desire for something to be different, then you must learn what you have not yet. Change will feel uncomfortable before it feels really good. Our brains, while neuroplastic and completely capable of change, resist having to forge a new pathway. That is all this is. Resistance. You can have resistance AND you can move towards change.

If you are ready to pick up the mantle of your feminine, then you must first learn the art of being magnetic and receiving so you are the energy that *pulls*, not the energy that pushes. That is all this is. Imagine when you master this art what you will do with it. How will your life change? How powerful will it feel to be able to flip between magnetic and boss-mode depending on what you need and want?

To be magnetic, you must get into the energetic vibration of that which you desire. If you desire to be desired, feel the energy of desire in your body – what creates this "type" of "bloom" within you? You desire to feel fun? Be the energy of play, fun and lightness – what creates this "type" of "bloom" within you?

Remember you are luminous, not illuminous. This is the self-responsible part where you claim your power. You do **not** need to wait for someone to initiate something in you, for you. You are fully capable of "hitting" all the chords of life-energy and energetically calling towards you the energetic match to that, taking you even deeper into feeling and sensation than you can take yourself. You go first; the universe responds. You must first put your "order in" with the universe, then adjust your order (energy) depending on what comes back.

The Goddess *invites*. When a flower penetrates (doing, telling, seeking an outcome), a mountain withdraws. When a flower invites, a mountain desires to go deeper into her, to penetrate her deeper than her heart and body can take itself. No different to the masseuse being able to massage you more deeply than you can massage yourself, and it feels *even* better. In the world of energy 1 + 1 = 3.

> *I had a great realisation this morning that I don't very often open up my presence to my husband – and of course I am always complaining about him being so distant and not "here." Of course*

he's distant, he can feel that I close off to him, and over the years he has "been trained" that he is not really wanted in my space. It pains me to say this, but I actually do this to my son also as he triggers me a lot and I am always trying to "get away" from these feelings and therefore close my energy, turn my back and move away from him in the home. This was a beautiful realisation for me and my practise this week is to open my body and heart to both of them whenever they are in my presence, intent to beam love from my heart and show them with my energy that they are welcome and wanted within my space … and then it dropped in. "My openness invokes his presence!"

– Tessa

You're always training him

You have a man as good at being in his masculine and handling feelings as you are in your feminine and handling her energy. So go gently. Remember, he's been trained for his entire life, as have you. Plus, for the amount of time you've been together, those patterns have been reinforced. So be gentle. With you, with him.

It will feel clunky before it feels smooth. It will feel uncomfortable before it becomes part of who you are and part of your new relationship dynamic.

When re-training him to know exactly what you're feeling:

- Don't delay the expression of your revealed heart or truth. Delay diminishes the energy's potency and therefore his presence. Work on "in the moment" responsiveness when he's hurt you or delighted you.
- No hiding, suppressing, repressing, holding on, clenching tightly – breathe, touch, soften, open, reveal your truth.
- Be a "yes" to whatever comes through your body, honouring when your heart hurts a little, letting him know and see it, so there's no guessing and he *can* course-correct.

This week with my husband has been incredible; we had a lovely date at home Friday night and another scheduled for tonight (we now have us literally booked into each other's diaries). He spent the whole weekend with us, choosing to do his work for his second job at our kitchen table instead of outside in his office which he would usually do. Did the dishes after every meal without my asking and cooked us pizzas for lunch. Brought home a bottle of red and a sexy movie suggestion on Friday … The changes after my being closer, honest and open with him has been breath-taking.

– Courtney

When working with your energy and working out how to flow with the energy that he pays attention to, go big before you go subtle. He needs to see the ripples or waves on the surface of the pond before he learns to read the subtler cues. You're training his sensitivity.

If he's been trained out of noticing any disturbance in you, his radar is weak; he won't notice subtle and you won't have learnt the art that is subtle. You need to re-learn your energy spectrum and movement within your body before you master how to move it more delicately but potently.

Yesterday my hubby and I hit another big one and after some big feeling releases from both of us we sat down and I asked him in desperation, "Just tell me how I can support you?! What does it look like? What do you want to hear in these times? How do I approach you?"

Then I sat back and listened as he stepped out pretty much EVERYTHING Julie had mentioned a week earlier to me. Meanwhile I'm sitting there with my jaw ON THE FLOOR and at one point I just burst into laughter and said, "I'm sorry to be laughing, I promise I'm listening to and loving and taking in everything you're saying- it's just that you're stepping out every single point Julie went over with me last week and it's like you've spoken with her and now I'm having a real life workshop!" It was AMAZING.

Without realising, he pretty much asked me to approach him totally in my feminine, to set the space up for him and invite him into it softly and gently, and swoon him back into safety and trust.

IT WAS LIKE YOU WERE IN MY LIVING ROOM, Julie, I literally cannot believe the genius of this all.

– Allyce

If you hold back your truth, you keep him in the dark. He can't know what he can't see. You are always training your partner to respond or not respond to you. Which are you choosing? Heart truth or smooth pond? Don't make the mistake of deciding he can't meet you if you've never shown him your truth or skilled him up on how to. Men stay in the dark when women keep them so.

Knowing how to stay open, especially under "imperfect" conditions, is an art. It's what we practise here. If you close, he is clueless on what you want and how you want it.

Here's an example of an interaction I had with my husband where my heart yearned for something to be experienced other than it was, and instead of collapsing, I *trained him* into how I wanted to experience life.

"You don't just take a coffee from a goddess." I smiled like a Cheshire cat as he took the coffee I'd bought him from my hand without acknowledgement.

It was a mini-hurt, but if I bury the small hurts, he never has the chance to learn how to behave (love me well) and respond to me differently; I become complicit in my own heart-abuse.

I "pulled him up" on what hurt but I did it with an open body and an inviting heart. *Try again; it will feel pleasure-full when you get it right,* my body said.

"Yes." He smiled as he walked slowly towards me, squaring the front of his body to match mine. Presence. I'm already swooning, so my body beckons that response; *right, keep going …*

"You take her as well," he said, half a question testing for my response, half a statement he knows so well.

My smile broadened. My body must have visibly swooned, though I couldn't say, as the honey-coloured feeling consumed me; all I could feel was his arm curl around the small of my back.

And it is here, in the middle of a shopping centre, we have an exceptionally erotic moment that fuels our day with energy and polarity.

You are always training your man. Always. Delicious surrender isn't a single moment at the end of a day. It's all the mini-moments that make up a day.

If you've cultivated your mountain more than your flower, you will have a false tendency to believe the only options are to penetrate and get your needs met or to withdraw because they never will be. There is another way.

First ask yourself: do you want to be the mountain or the flower in this moment? Which response do you want to evoke in your partner?

In every moment, YOU GET TO CHOOSE. You are not at the mercy of life, love and people *outside* of you. **You. Are. Life.** Take back your power. In *any* moment, **you can choose.**

If you want to feel *more* and be penetrated by him, his consciousness, his body or his presence, get in your feminine! He won't be the one penetrating if you're the one in the masculine. He'll be opening or closing. The moment you're more energy, more feeling and more feminine polarity than him is the exact moment his masculine energy springs to life and you get what you want!

If you want to be the one in charge, taking him and his feelings, then keep penetrating and holding the masculine polarity. He'll surrender to you instead.

You always get to choose.

Desire

He's in his feminine but
you want to be

Holding feminine polarity

Masculine energy adores "taking" their lover. Feminine energy craves to be "taken" by their lover.

The mountain *loves* to make the flower swoon so she releases into deeper energy. The pleasure is not found in *creating it* for himself. The more the flower moves, the stiller the mountain becomes, the more focused his attention and presence. *She* becomes his purpose for existing, his reason to be *here* (in his body, not his mind), his altar to *worship* at. The pleasure for the flower is found in his strong presence and attention directed onto her, where she's able to swoon, feel more and be worshipped like the Goddess she is.

> *My husband always says that some of his favourite memories of me are when he has seen me dancing and how it makes me glow.*
>
> – Meagan

Feminine energy is the elixir of life. The Holy Grail. As a flower ripples energy through her body in response to a stimulus, it creates a tidal wave of energy that quakes and shakes the very centre of the mountain, which he *cannot* ignore. No matter his current single focus, if it is the energy that excites and stimulates his otherwise bland "nothingness," or on a subconscious level he registers that it will enliven and rejuvenate him from his intense focus, he's in, hook, line and sinker (revisit "When your interruption from his single focus feels good").

I just tried polarity practice in the bakery, with two men, it was instant! They also went from dead still standing, heads in phones, to looking straight at me, and they couldn't stop moving and being fidgety as I continued to stand there. Haha, it was magic to watch, blown away! I had to stop doing it as I felt bad for their wanting and them not knowing what was happening hahaha.

– Pamela

Men love an "object of desire." Women love to "be the object of desire." Obviously, the more strongly you sit in either energy will determine the more strongly you align with this statement, but it is true nonetheless and the crux of desire within a couple.

You can have love *and* you can have desire the moment you realise you can animate these energetic-extremes at will – any time you want it, like within the bedroom when we're wanting to spark intense energy and chemistry between you. For the rest of your life, when you're running a business, a household and a gaggle of children, you may be quite content being sexually neutral. Wonderful! Just know you have the power to change the energy within you, your partner and the room at will, any time you choose.

Throughout your day, life and sex together, both of you, flower and mountain, will want to switch polarity and animate your opposite energy state. The mountain will want to let go and feel, and the flower will want to lead. This can feel wonderful, novel and playful – so long as it is a conscious *choice* that takes you both into a richer experience of self and other. If it becomes a *habituated* way of being, *with no alternative*, it will become repulsive.

Polarity as it already exists within your relationship

The cosmic joke in relationship is "that which initially attracts you will become that which repels you." Likely, initially you adored how "opposite" your partner was to you.

If you reject your feminine:
- He's emotional; you're rational
- He has no direction, likes to "go with the flow"; you need structure and goals
- He loves fashion and his beauty; you love black and prefer "no frosting"
- He likes to talk and feel; you withdraw

If you reject your masculine:
- He doesn't know how to talk about feelings, is super rational or leaves the conversation; you want to talk every minute detail to death
- You flow, feel, don't complete and move to the new shiny thing; he sets targets and doesn't change till he's reached them
- He's distant "nothingness"; you're red-hot energy and emotion
- He's happy in any old thing or black; you adore colour, lip gloss, all the things!

This polarity and energetic dynamic you have may still be working super well for you. If it is, then disregard this section! If it's stopped working, then you're being asked to empower the energy that you have previously "outsourced."

To add context here, let's look back at why I chose the lovers I did. Let's consider that what initially was a source of attraction for both of us became the very thing that was repulsive. When it became repulsive, I claimed those traits for *myself* and no longer needed to outsource them to these lovers.

Among my first relationship rodeos were two equal and opposite experiences: the Italian feminine-energy lover and the masculine-energy shadow warrior.

The Italian lover

I sigh when I think about how beautiful he was. So beautiful. An Adonis, with the soul of a poet and the heart of a lover. I mean, really. I was helpless. The trouble was, he was more emotional than I was. He cried more freely than I did. He was more exuberant than I allowed myself to be. He cared more about his appearance and beauty than he cared about mine. It's perfect. Equal and opposite. Can you see it?

While I had a feminine incarnation, I had learnt in childhood to hide and suppress those traits; so wounded was I, I rejected all of my feminine charms. I wondered if perhaps I was gay. I had an exceptionally well-cultivated masculine. Internally, I could out-man most men. I delighted in feminine form. I absorbed her energy like it was my life force because, when I was animating so much masculine, it was. I SO get, in a really tangible way, why women are so magnificent to behold and how you feel blessed by their energy. How watching her ravishment of a moment enlivens you instantaneously, how she is intoxicating to breathe in and receive.

So here I was. Feminine shell, masculine animated interior. I attracted my equal and opposite. A masculine shell, feminine animated interior. It was perfect. Until it wasn't. Then I was called into growth.

His feminine became repulsive to me. *I* wanted to take up that space. In actuality, I was repulsed by *me and my own rejection of my feminine,* but I cast that outward, and *he* became the source of my repulsion. I wanted what he had. I wanted it for me, not via him. I was ready to reclaim it. Though at the time I was not aware this was what was happening and he just pissed me off.

Repulsion forces your energy back into yourself, where otherwise your energy would move outward into another person. Repulsion's purpose is *for* your own growth.

I realise this could be triggering for some readers, so please skip this section and move on if you have triggers around violence and abuse.

The shadow warrior

The next man I exchanged polarity with was a mountain of a man. Strong. Sure of himself. Solid. My father had just passed away. So blocked was my feminine in my home, I couldn't cry if I *tried*. And believe me, I tried. I was numb. Empty. So I found a man who was an even stronger warrior than I was. One who could out-masculine me. When what I craved was my surrender rather than my control, I found a man who could *make* me feel and surrender. Equal and opposite. Always trying, however obscured, to reclaim our wholeness.

So mountain was this man, he was almost completely devoid of emotion. So empty. So still. A "nothingness" I craved. He was equally my salvation from my emotionally charged home and so "empty" that even I had more energy than him. I could experience my feminine around this masculine. He out-masculined me. His strong masculine "forced" me into my feminine and I started feeling again.

Yes, it came in shadow form. But this man, even through his abuse of my body, made me feel again. He cracked through my tough shells of protection. They were glass to him. He bent the oak-like pillar at the centre of me. He shook the hardened debris from my body. He took when I was unwilling to give. He forced my surrender, and I was a warrior. But the relief. I was addicted. The relief I felt at feeling. I can never explain to you how that felt. To be so "battered" out of your natural state as a child, you become a false type of hard, only to discover you were water at your source. It was literally intoxicating. He was my drug. Around him, I remembered. Even if it was in shadow. I remembered.

Slowly, I reclaimed. My hurting heart started to move in motion *with* MY inner masculine, no longer *separated*. The more I "married" my own feminine and masculine, the less I needed him, until one day, in a movie-drama style moment, I said, "No. No more," and my sister swooped in between him and I. Her ferocity and certainty completed whatever masculine I was missing in that moment, and he left.

And then I healed.
And then I understood.
And then I surrendered open to the divine. I felt forgiveness. I felt grace.
I reclaimed my power.

And then I met my now husband.

I will add that this is a simplistic version of this dynamic. When in a committed relationship, obviously you're not ending it and separating, so the choice becomes to reclaim polarity within the relationship, which is the practise my husband and I now have.

Leading

Leading, taking charge of direction, space, time and everyone within it is a masculine energy superpower. This is why motherhood is a masculine energy. If you are a strong leader, this polarity will be strong within you and work magnificently well in your office, but it is death for sexual chemistry with a mountain. (Of course, if you're wanting to ignite chemistry with a flower energy, it's perfect.)

Your mountain wants you to feel his presence, his strength, to trust his direction, his thoughts and ideas for leading a better life, now and in the future.

A flower loves being led and having someone take charge because it allows her to be full energy, present in every moment because someone else has charge of safety and direction.

It feels good for a mountain to say "come," and his flower moves in response. This flower moves with delight because she knows she'll feel *even* better when she does, or she doesn't like his direction and still feels better because she's free-responding energy and knows he'll course-correct to meet her desires.

Don't get stuck in the mindset of *I won't do what a man tells me* – if you are in a loving relationship, this is a polarity *practice*, not a place of staying all the time. Polarity is fluid and will switch between partners. Sometimes you'll want to lead, sometimes he'll want to follow and vice versa; it is simply that whoever identifies more strongly with either energy will enjoy the traits and sexual play inherent to that energy more thoroughly.

It feels delicious to your mountain when you trust him, his direction and ability to lead. Just as it feels delicious for you, flower, to be absolved of "what next," to be able to have "pockets" of space and time to completely let go of control, organising and "management" and instead bloom into delight and surrender. It's rejuvenating for both of you.

Flower, please practise letting your mountain lead, by letting go.

Letting go means letting go of the need for life to flow as *you* wish it to (control, direction, masculine force) and surrendering to the desire present in each moment, because if he doesn't get his leadership exactly right, you don't have to *tell* him what to do or how to do it; he can do that for himself. He's a big boy. You just have to *feel* and *amplify* the energy of what you are already feeling, which feels like release and ecstasy.

> *So many things have hit me like a ton of bricks actually. There have been times when I have muttered to myself "you are hopeless," a whole story around him "not being handy," around him "being useless." I'm even a bit embarrassed to write that as I realise all the ways I've actually projected these things on to him and haven't allowed him to step into his masculine.*
>
> *I watched the live training [from Julie's relationship program] and then cried and cried, my husband Matt came in and said "what's wrong?" and I said, "I'm just really sad." He held me while I cried, which he has done before; I felt the grief and pain. I felt like I could have cried for ages, and even writing this I feel it. Towards the end I said to him that "I love when you hold me" and he said, "I love holding you," which made me cry some more. I also sobbed that I*

was sorry for all the times I haven't seen him and have cut him off at the knees, and that I'm learning to see him in a whole new way and love him more deeply. I could feel this seep into him.

– Shelley

Letting go can happen in small ways. It doesn't have to look like a big, grand gesture. In fact, I'd advise the smaller the better. It's the small changes that will help you build trust in him to step forward and trust in you to let go of the reins one at a time.

When you're used to being in charge and your partner is used to going with the flow, it will take some new learning. You're asking yourself to *step back* from leading and into being led (move into feminine receiving), and you're asking your partner to *step up* from being led to being the one who's leading (move into masculine leading).

When learning to hold a new polarity, you have to allow your partner time to flounder in their direction and work out what they simply haven't had to before, because you've always done it for them and taken the lead! His struggle (stress) is a beautiful thing; he's reclaiming his masculine polarity! Stay open and in feeling, stay in your feminine polarity, and I promise you he will meet you in exactly the way you crave but couldn't articulate. Just like this couple did:

Every year we go away for a weekend. Usually I book. This time I wanted him to. To surprise me. Organise everything. He did. So sexy. Super hot. There were times I witnessed him trying to push me into my masculine by asking me where I wanted to go, where he should book and to basically book it.

He told me it was stressing him out as he was worried he wouldn't please me etc. And could I book or suggest something.

It was so hard for me not to jump in and rescue him. I so wanted to take over and book but I didn't. I just knew that wherever he booked, wherever it was, it would be perfect because he booked it!

I also told myself wherever he booked I would be grateful, super appreciative and not be critical at all!

Turns out, not an issue. He booked us the perfect place. He blew me away with how he handled this – a man who has never booked a place in his life (I always do it) and a man who is super tight and hates spending money booked a fancy hotel.

So much love.

The entire drive to our destination (which I asked him not to tell me) was a mystery. The whole drive I couldn't take the smile off my face. I had no idea where we were going; I was being whisked away.

I felt so loved. And realised this is something I have desired MY ENTIRE life but never asked for.

To be taken away. To not book something. For a man to whisk me away, pack everything, plan everything and all I need do is get in the car and be taken.

The whole time I was feeling the energy in my body. Like really feeling it, and enjoying the sensations of excitement and joy. I was in tears with it all.

To sum up, our desires and feeling them in every part of our body is powerful.

– Nicole

If you crave a partner who can swoop in and say "baby, pack your bags for cold weather. We leave at 5pm," instead of "I don't know, we'll do whatever you want to do," then your practise begins here.

Where does polarity exist in humans?

This universe is constructed on opposites that create forces. Like a battery, a positive and negative charge creates an arc of electricity. Difference creates the spark of attraction; a positive and a negative charge irresistibly attracted to each other form an electrically charged current that powers any system. For humans, it is the same. When opposite energetic forces meet, we receive an "electrical jolt" to our system, felt as attraction, desire, infatuation. When two of the same forces meet, there is either a repulsion (like a magnet), or neutrality (no spark, no desire).

Positive poles penetrate the world or another person with energy. Negative poles are where energy is received.

The energetic positive and negative poles exist in opposite locations on the human body for flowers and mountains (regardless of gender):

Positive pole (where energy penetrates):
Flower – her heart/breast space
Mountain – his genitals

Negative pole (where energy is received):
Flower – her genitals
Mountain – his heart/chest space

This is powerful information to know. It is in actuality where the old adage comes from: "men need sex for connection, women need connection for sex" – because it's **all about** the poles!

Positive pole stimulation sends energy *into* our negative pole. When a positive pole is stimulated to the point of this "overflow," we find our negative pole is "juiced up" and ready to be penetrated: mentally, emotionally, energetically or physically.

A man's positive pole is his genitals. When the penis is the focus of stimulation, the energy overflows into his negative pole: his heart space. Stimulation of his penis opens his energy, which flows towards his heart. Hence, men need sex for connection.

A woman's positive pole is her heart and breast space. When this area is the focus of stimulation FOR her, following *her* unfolding and desire expanding, not porno-style boob grabs that close her heart (though sometimes you might be up for this!), the energy overflows into her negative pole: her genitals – turning her on and increasing wetness. Hence, women need heart-connection for sex.

Unfortunately, this is a little-known fact. Plus, women tend not to train their men into what makes a good lover *for* them, and often fall into habituated patterns of performance and "putting up" with mediocre, average or completely unpresent sex.

Men, completely unaware and likely only "trained" by porn and their own years of tension-filled, heart-closed masturbation, continue with what they know, believing it is good sex. His presence remains shallow; her heart remains closed. Both of them miss out. She "thickens up." Her Goddess-given ability to feel ecstasy in the subtle is dulled out of her, until it's only a vibrator she can feel or her vagina is numb; her wetness dries up and achieving orgasm is off the table or reduced to a set of predictable steps.

It is this misunderstanding that creates the old "crotch-grab" most women abhor. Yet it seems to be the go-to for most men to initiate sex, assuming (wrongly) that as his positive pole "lubes him up" for sex, it will do the same for her.

He DOESN'T KNOW your positive pole exists somewhere else, and if you go straight for a negative pole, it creates closure, not opening. Please, please, please, tell him! Tell him, it feels great to be touched "there" after you're *overflowing* with energy, opened into desire, *craving* to be touched or penetrated. Spend WAY more time stroking, kissing and stimulating your whole breast/chest/décolletage/neck area. Slow down. Ask him to only touch or penetrate when *you* ask for it!

Please wait for your body. Wait for your wetness. Keep exploring until "she" flows. Not wet yet? Not ready yet. Be patient with your body while you learn a new language; she's worth waiting for. Start to shift what good sex means for you.

Remember, flower: the degree to which you animate your flower or mountain will be the reciprocal degree to which your partner animates the opposite. The more opposite, the more attraction is present. The more same, the less attraction or repulsion. That's polarity. To experience something other than you are, put yourself in the polarity you wish to experience – giving (masculine) or receiving (feminine) – and you will automatically "push" your partner into the opposite force to the same degree, changing your sexual play.

Polarity practice

This is your practice: how long can you hold the polarity of the feminine for? Long enough for him to work out what to do and deliver it to you? Or will you collapse your practice earlier than he has a chance to meet you?

The practice of "taking up space," "pushing him out of his feminine" and holding your own state, is big work. That's why self-practice first, partner-practice second. Revisit the section "How to establish your feminine practice" if you need a refresher. Your best practice is exactly what is coming up for you now, in your body.

Ask:
What is coming up for me now?
How can I make this feel even better?
How can I amplify it?

Anticipate difficulty! Don't collapse and give up when it gets hard. If it were easy, you wouldn't be learning anything! This is hard *because* you're learning! Let it be playful; he's your barometer for how you're going with your energy. If he hasn't noticed yet, don't give up! Do all the things you need to feel the energy you want to feel more thoroughly. You'll know when you've nailed it because he'll give you exactly the response you're after.

You have to be willing to practise every day. Don't collapse when it doesn't work or you mess it up. You're learning a new language. Give yourself time. You have to learn the characters that make up the alphabet. Then the colloquial exchanges, conversational and structural sentence formats, before it becomes easeful.

It's learning a new language.

It's visiting a new country.

It's understanding their customs.

Give yourself time, patience and self-compassion as you unlearn to re-learn.

So yesterday was a bit shit and I was really cranky with myself by the end of the day for not using everything I've learnt. I've been working really hard on communication and opening. Hubby and I have had some great conversations over the past few weeks and when either of us has shut down (we're both scared of conflict so tend to go icy or shut down and are working on this) I've been able to fight internally with myself and break the ice and guide us through some awkward but beautiful conversations.

But yesterday I just stayed stuck. From first thing in the morning I had all the old stories come up and the tension kept building throughout the day. I had extra kids to look after and he had house fixing stuff to do so we both went about our business. By the evening I snapped over something minor and he tried to container me by doing all the things I've asked him to do in previous conversations, but I was having none of it. I chose to stay closed and angry. Then I was more angry and sad that I'd chosen that. I wanted to apologise once I'd calmed down but he was asleep. So this morning I sent this message and got this response:

"Hello sweetheart. I'm sorry. You didn't deserve that treatment. I appreciate that you tried. I'm still upset but wanted to apologise for not addressing things earlier in the day. By last night I was too far gone and there wasn't anything you could do to help. I hope you have a good day xo"

"Please don't apologise, I should have been paying more attention to your needs earlier in the day. I accept 100% responsibility for my role. I love you and am trying to be better."

It made me laugh. It made me cry.

I just wanted to share as I know Julie talks about how important it is to express ourselves in real time and I'm really trying to but it's HARD and sometimes I fail. But rather than giving up in this case and seeing a missed opportunity, I'm looking at where I can learn from this and grow through it for next time. I hope that this is what Julie means by practice. We're not going to want to do the hard work in the moment 100% of the time, or even get it right if we do try, but I can choose to take 100% responsibility for what happened and what happens next (although in this instance it seems he is taking 100% responsibility also).

I guess what I'm saying is, I'm grateful for second chances and so grateful for this work. I know some of us feel like we'll never find this as easy as Julie does, but I have so much love and admiration for myself and each of you beautiful women for us being here and being willing to do the work and grow.

– Lauren

His presence matches your energy

If you are the flower or wanting to be, your responsibility is energy. If you are the mountain or seeking to be, your responsibility is presence. At any moment, either of you can influence the other into a stronger energic pole by consciously taking up a stronger polarity at either end of the spectrum (masculine or feminine).

Less polarity = less energy (feminine) and less attention (masculine).

Your degree of *feminine* evokes his degree of *masculine* and vice versa.

> *It's easy to see when we're both in these energies. It's allowing myself to slip easily into my feminine when I want him to be in his masculine … this is still a practice, trying to get through his density and switch off my masculine … but the times it does happen it's amazing! Everything just happens, he's on purpose and his capacity to hold a lot of energy is beautiful.*
>
> – Bronwyn

This is powerful when you realise:
If you meet him in your masculine energy, you will evoke his feminine. He'll want to snuggle, talk, hang out … but he won't make moves. He will want to "be taken" by you.

If you meet him in a neutral energy, you will be neutral together. You'll be friends, but your body won't "turn on."

If you meet him in your feminine, you will evoke his masculine. He'll be seeking to talk less and enjoy making you swoon, desiring to "enter you" (emotionally, energetically, physically).

You get to choose. In any moment, you get to choose. When you know what you desire and get yourself in that energy, what you desire becomes a reality.

Want a bestie, be the same.
Want to be ravished, be feminine.

But don't wish for something, make no action towards it and then get cranky and upset you didn't get what you wished for. The universe and all its governing forces of attraction respond to intention + inspired action.

I practise this all the time now, though I didn't before. I used to believe that his "floppiness" on the couch and missing of my seemingly "obvious" hints meant either I was undesirable, or I had married a man who had no interest in sex or in creating sexual chemistry. All were crushing thoughts for me.

I tried pleasing myself without him, but this only led to my building more resentment towards him and more disconnection between us.

I stacked the evidence that he was disappointing and I couldn't have what I wanted with him. The more I decided this, the more self-sufficient I became. The less I needed him, the less room there was for him to show up. I was my own husband, but still I was unfulfilled.

I tried having "conscious," somewhat defensive conversations with him about it, but it always seemed to "die out" and we were back to where we started. I remember the heaviness at feeling entirely responsible for our sex life.

What I was missing was polarity. I met him with my masculine mind, but I didn't surrender to my own feminine. I pushed, but I didn't pull. I met him in neutrality (zero sexual chemistry) or in aggression and hurt; I didn't surrender my masculine polarity, and by virtue of that he stayed in his feminine.

Now, when I feel a desire for desire and a craving "to be taken," I turn my energy inward towards my own feminine. When I'm the honey, he can't help being the bee that is magnetically attracted. I focus on giving myself everything I need to flow with feminine-honey, knowing this is my secret to feeling fulfilled, to having whatever I want (him included) and to moving through my day with my kids in ease and joy. Truly.

My desire to be desired is **my** reminder to get into my feminine. I dress for my own desire. I eat for my own desire. I move with my own desire. It's a glorious next-level self-care practice. The more I flow, the more his attention is upon me. It's a win-win.

We all outsource what the relationship doesn't provide

The masculine in all of us seeks to be replenished by the feminine. If masculine is expending, feminine is replenishing, and we all need both.

If within the couple, your feminine energy is not free-flowing, your partner will seek for it outside of the relationship. As will you when you are the masculine energy within the relationship.

The feminine exists as matter (energy/atoms create matter). Anything that has form and has a sensual component to its experience is inherently feminine. Our partners will experience their feminine "revitalisation" via us or they'll outsource it:

- TV
- Beer
- Fishing
- Golfing
- Tussling with nature and the wild

- Walks and runs on the beach
- Swimming
- His car ...

A man in his boat, tussling with the wildness of the ocean, receives feminine replenishment. He reads her currents, works out how to penetrate her waves and glide over her surface. He feels revitalised.

A man walking down the beach, feeling the wind rush through his hair and sweep over his body, clearing his mind and relaxing his muscles, feels renewed.

A man who enters nature's rugged forest, seeks to find himself in her wilderness, to experience all of her elements, to meet the edges of who he is and survive in response to her, feels enlivened.

A man who admires the grace and beauty of his car, slides his hands over her curves, lusciously rubs her behind, tenderly caresses her every crevice until she's glowing, feels that brightness within his own heart and body.

> *My partner's outlet is cleaning, waxing, and buffing his car every single free day he has. If he feels more tension or needs time out, he's back to his car. He's refuelled by it. Now I get it.*
>
> – Nicole

If your feminine has been shut down for a while, he may have outsourced his feminine nourishment. At times this may feel really good for you! It certainly does for me sometimes! I fully enjoy receiving feminine energy nourishment from sources outside of my relationship, as does my husband, and while that works for you there is nothing to change.

When you crave a little more attention and seek more connection with him, you *can* reclaim that space any time. Reclaiming that space will begin with radical self-ownership of your feminine polarity.

The flow of energy equals the flow of presence. If you were at a busy restaurant and a singer was covered in sequins, throwing him or herself all over the stage and singing their heart out, would you leave your dinner conversation to watch? If you were at a busy restaurant and they had a little mouse of a singer in the back corner, would you leave your dinner conversation to watch?

This is not to cast blame or shame; this is just interesting. Humans are curious. The more you awaken curiosity within *your* mind, heart and body, the more interesting the person in front of you becomes! You can train your brain to be interested in anything! Whatever you focus your interest on becomes interesting, and by virtue of that, hormones of intrigue and novelty begin to accumulate in your system, igniting chemistry. Likely, that's exactly what your chosen interests do.

Get curious about human behaviour. Get curious about his and you'll see it. The moment you do, this gets to inform all your previous conceptions, ideas and beliefs. Is it true he's genuinely more interested in his car or work than you? Which one has more energy right now? Do *you* want his attention? Change your energy and he will give you what you want. Show less energy and he'll focus on his car or work. Show more energy than his work or car and he'll focus on you.

Same for you. Sometimes your partner or child will be more interesting to you than your work or activity, and sometimes they won't be. It's all energy-flow.

Energy through your body is a win-win.

Relationship

Where it gets tricky

Some mountains have a very low bandwidth for tolerating flower feeling states. However, we cannot love *only* the parts of the flower that are convenient for us; it is the cracks in the crystal through which the sun reflects the most beautiful rainbows. Instead, we need to learn how to tussle with the wildishness of the feminine and her "storms." It is the key to an ecstatic relationship.

Some mountains have not had good experiences being raised by flowers and do not trust their ways; they reject the flower *within* them *and* outside of them (see feminine rejection). This mountain has developed a decreased emotional bandwidth *inwardly*, and his tolerance *outwardly* is equally diminished.

This mountain sits so far in the masculine pole of "nothingness" that if you are anything more than nothing, it is deeply uncomfortable for him. He will seek *more* freedom and release from the tension *any* feeling causes. The greater the feeling, the greater the need for him to be free from it.

These mountains won't try; they'll withdraw because they've already decided it can't be fixed and they don't know how.

This is a man who craves to be intimate with the Goddess but who rejects her at the same time, wishing he could have the bits he desires (that make him feel enlivened) but that she be "a monk in a monastery" the rest of the time, which of course is not possible for a feminine flower.

These mountains ask their flower to thicken, to suppress her flow in order to be more still because he cannot handle her as she is. He asks her to deviate from her true nature, in order to take a shape more tolerable to him. It is a great sadness to ask a flower to be less flower and more mountain.

Possibly the greatest travesty of all is that the more still she becomes, the less erotic she will become, for there is less life coursing through her body. Be careful what you ask for, mountain.

You cannot spend a lifetime telling a flower her natural form is *wrong*, coercing her to change shape, to suppress, to control, to restrict – then tell her to "turn it on" *now* that you want sex or energy. It is an atrocity the Goddess recoils from in horror to witness. It is possibly the deepest wound of the feminine, for her energy to become a commodity to control and a force to be given or taken, as opposed to a blessing to receive and an altar to worship at.

The trouble is this mountain genuinely doesn't know what to do with you when "you're like this." He literally has no other options or skills. In this case, you need to drop *any* assumptions you have about what he knows or isn't willing to do and begin at kindergarten-level with a how-to guide on "handling you."

This is not scolding him and telling him what to do like his mother. This is his Goddess *showing* him what feels good and how he *can* succeed.

You need to take him on a tour as his guide *and* give him your how-to manual. **Each emotion needs its own guide:**
- Hold me like this …
- Say these words …
- Don't do this …

- Do this ...

If you could literally answer these questions under "section titles" for each of your emotional states, it would be immensely helpful for him and immensely freeing for you. Yes, this is a masculine style of communication, but when training the masculine outside of you how to handle you at your most vulnerable (when you are emotionally open), it is important to communicate in black and white with no assumptions. It is the time spent in creating this safety that will allow your feminine emotions to flow with ease and healing.

So you can be more feminine energy, let him know that you take full responsibility for how you feel and if what's happening doesn't feel good that you'll let him know and guide him in working out how to meet you. He can't lose. And neither can you.

You may even like to tell him what you're seeking out of an interaction (what the goal is) as you learn.

I just need you to listen and tell me ... (give him specific words you need to hear to help you release).

This is about you swooning and softening by constantly checking in with yourself:

- Is this exactly the sweet spot that I'm craving to feel?
- Is this absolutely satisfying and I feel like I can let go?
- If not, what do I need? what needs to change?

Reveal more and more energy in small amounts each time you practise together, "testing" his ability to handle you and tussle with your emotions. Trusting his ability to lead, letting go of leadership in small amounts. As he builds his skills and his confidence, you'll build your ability to release more and more energy, until eventually you'll stop needing to guide him and he'll start leading you instead.

Don't make the mistake of throwing him your "tornado" and expecting him to hold it from the very beginning. Slow, gentle, compassionate practice is needed for both of you. As you practise revealing and owning your own feelings *through* your body, his equal and opposite practice will be learning how to "hold you" and be with emotions and energy that he never has before.

We think we're seeking his passion, but really we're seeking depth and presence

When a flower feels a lack of love-flow, when she feels her partner is unpresent or leaving her in some respect, she will pick an experience of energy-flow *over* its absence, she will initiate a fight. She will prod in exactly the right ways in order to elicit presence from her mountain. In her body, *any* energy is better than none.

For a mountain, an argument and big emotional charge are something to move on from so he can return to "life." He will always seek its conclusion. For a flower, the argument and all the currents of energy, attention and focus, *ARE* life for her. She wants to stay where the energy and presence are.

When we do this unconsciously, we miss the opportunity to evoke polarity and have an ecstatic energy-exchange with our lover. Have you ever or do you ever prod your partner to elicit an argument?

Is there a part of you that knows this energy exchange feels better than the absence of energy between you?

Is there a part of you that "enjoys" his attention during an argument?

> *Yes THIS IS ME. In my wounded space I totally prod him. When I feel like a certain amount of time has passed and I perceive he has been withdrawn and shut off from me I definitely have a tendency to want to poke the sleeping bear back into MY SPHERE ... Yes – at least then I've got SOME presence and attention ... Even if I've clawed it out. OUCH. That's a painful one to admit but also love that my partner and I can laugh about this wounded child part of me.*
>
> > – Allyce

> *Yep! I would rather an argument over him shutting down or tuning me out. Guilty. I guess I prefer angry attention, argument attention to being ignored, shut out.*
>
> > – Wendy

> *I am a military spouse so have a partner that has to go away a lot, sometimes at short notice and for long periods. It's well known in the military community that spouses often pick fights with the serving member in the days before they leave ... I always thought it was a way of "disconnecting" from them, but perhaps it actually is the opposite, and is more about trying to maximise their attention!*
>
> > – Meagan

Consider being savvier in how you elicit his presence and ignite energy between you by getting in your feminine and honouring what it is your heart *truly* yearns to feel and experience.

She craves your presence (masculine practice)

She craves to be seen, heard, felt and touched. Everywhere. Her surfaces and her heart, mind and soul.

This can sound hard, but really it isn't.

In your masculine, find the place within you that is still. Come into as much calm stillness as you possibly can.

Get your feet firmly on the ground, feel like the mountain – strong, grounded, bigger than any wind current.

Square your shoulders.

Face your chest to hers. This is important. If you're slumped or slightly turned away from her, she can't feel your presence and she'll punish you for it. She'll be irritated as you appear physically as though "you can't meet her" and she'll close off her heart to you.

Breathe deeply. Never stop focusing on your breath being deep and slow. You can actually soothe her by breathing deeply.

If you lead with your depth (stillness), strength (posture) and breath, she will eventually fall into your groundedness. She will match your regulation and it will feel delicious to her.

Track the edges of her body with your eyes.

Focus on something you can love about her in this moment: her eye colour, the softness of her skin, her passionate heart.

Listen. Nothing to fix. Nothing to change here. She will actually self-resolve without you doing anything other than this. So kick back and chill. Wait with presence for the energy moving through her to be fully felt and dissolved. Your life will be harder if you try to stop this energy moving through or try to mould it into being something other than it is.

This is the "easiest" work you will ever do. Do *nothing* but feel into your stillness and her heart. Breathe.

Let this energy roll, like a wave. Be the surfer who enjoys riding the power and force of the wave, knowing it's a short-lived exhilaration because as the wave reaches the shore, the ride is over. The surfer doesn't need to do anything to the wave for it to end, does he?

Same with women and emotion. Don't do anything. Just surf the wave. Hold strong and deep and empty, knowing this is the best medicine you can offer her and when you do, she will naturally dissolve this wave and move towards you in love.

Flowers test, mountains align

Flowers test their mountains to keep him sharp, present and at his masculine best. Without this "testing," he may become flaccid in his attention and presence, diminishing both him and her.

Like the goddess you are, you will set up traps for your mountain to walk *into*. In an Indiana Jones-style setup, you'll booby-trap the temple to ensure only those worthy reach your treasure. And you will test *constantly* to see: will he rise, succeed and claim you?

Through her testing, she offers him ways of building his masculine core, of developing his gifts and influence, of strengthening his spine, worth and ability to provide, if he chooses to take her testing as such. A lesser man will collapse instead. He'll give up. Call a truce flag. Slump away. He may stay as he is, but he won't grow in his masculine or his ability to tussle with the feminine.

The masculine in all of us sees the world in right/wrong, black/white, perfect/imperfect, success/failure. The mountain within you seeks to keep your actions in integrity. To keep your light in focus. Your inner mountain is always doing just this: critiquing, refining, offering something *better*, so too is your external mountain.

Just like you want your mountain to grow "better" or more capable by virtue of being able to "handle more" from your testing, so too is the mountain wanting to grow you, flower, to ensure your light is not wasted, that it is directed with purpose and integrity.

Will you let his "perfecting" (offering structure) raise you in the same way? Or will you reject his desire to offer alignment? Will you see it as an act of love or another way "you're not good enough?"

If it's not the right kind of alignment, if he's missed the kind of structure you need, will you tell him? Will you show him? Will you stay open to him while he reorients and delivers what you need?

You are always training each other.

Bypassing intimacy, stop assuming, start sharing

Expectations are the cause of suffering, not reality itself. Suffering occurs when you have an attachment to a "fantasy future" which our partner hasn't been clued-in on and fails to meet.

Assumptions lead to expectations not being met. The stuff we "assume" is the stuff we'd rather "brush over" or bypass instead of dig into.

Assumptions go like this:
- He does know ...
- He should know ...
- It's so obvious!
- I've even given him all the clues and hints
- He is ...
- He isn't ...
- He will ...
- He won't ...
- He'll say/do/think ...
- I already know how it's going to go ...
- The truth of who he is as **I** see him
- The truth of who I am is as **I** see it
- The truth of what is happening in our relationship "below the surface" is as **I** know it to be ...

Assumptions are the belief that reality is as *you* see it; you know everything about everyone else involved in that presumed reality.

You've decided what they do know, don't know, how they will act, react, think, feel and believe in this fantasy future. None of which are true. We are complicated humans, with complicated inner realities.

Assumptions are a bypass of intimacy practice. They are a lost opportunity that keeps you both playing small. What you resist persists until you willingly grow through it and open up to more love. The moment you stop assuming, you open up an entirely new, possible reality. Remember, you keep your partner clued-in or clueless.

Even after 20 years together, I know there's so much left to discover about this man I've shared a life with – because I know how much more there is to discover about myself. We are deep, complicated and mysterious beings. Vast and limitless. We can only ever know as much about a person as the amount of ocean that can be seen from the shore.

Any time you realise you're holding onto resentment or frustration with your partner, or are feeling rejected and unmet, ask yourself:
- What am I hurting (or insert feeling state) about?
- Can my hurt be traced back to feeling let down from an assumption I was holding about how this "should" have played out?
- Did I make any assumptions about what my partner might need (or not need) to be able to provide that?

Thinking about the assumptions you made:
- Instead of "leaping over" these "sticky bits," what would you need to do to clue him in on the pieces he doesn't know (that you assume he does) and ask for what you truly desire?
- When thinking about the actual conversation needed to clue him in, in excruciating detail (leave no assumptions) and ask him his in return, what fears come up?

Can you see how assumption is a creative way of avoiding the thing you're scared of? When we go below assumption, we awaken the opportunity to let go of a fear driving our behaviour and cheating us out of richer intimacy.

- What do you need to be able to show up with your partner in total truth and honesty?

One of the best things I ever did with my husband was share the "inner workings" of my mind, as a way of "clueing him in" but also as a way of "rewiring" my brain to a different reality to the one I'd learnt in childhood. It looked something like this:

Me, registering flashing anger at his response: "Okay, so when you just … I felt … and then my mind went … and I believe it means you think I'm …"

Him, genuinely shocked and in disbelief: "Umm, no. I meant what I said. I don't think any of those things. I really mean … "

Me: "Really?"

Him: "Yes. Really. I mean what I say, there's no reading between lines necessary."

Me: "Okay. I'll breathe that in."

I work on softening, *receiving* his words into my heart, being willing to see the world and me as he does. I ask him to repeat any words of affirmation I need to continue softening open. Sometimes I need to hear the same sentence ten times until I feel it "land" in my body!

The moment you offer him the opportunity to reveal *his* reality and help you soften yours (by letting go of your wounded beliefs and opening up to his words and intent), you're freed from the self-created glass ceiling and self-sabotage you're living.

Get on the same team

When we change the rules, you have to be willing to be with your own practice of polarity and wait for him to orient towards you. It will take time. You may feel frustrated. You may want to yell, turn his head for him, flip him out of his seat. Don't. What he doesn't learn for *himself* is not valued. Trust his masculine, trust your feminine light. Work on all the beliefs that come up as you orient to being a magnetic light and wait for him to connect to it.

I often think of this like teaching my children to read. When my child brings home a reader, I am the sun and they are the flower. This is a new skill, not yet mastered, for the flower. Each time my child stumbles on a word or doesn't understand a letter, do I slam the book closed and scream at them, "You're so stupid! You're never going to get it! There's no point!?"

Nope. If I did that, my child would never learn to read.

I stay, beaming light, love and patience. I wait for them to get it. I might offer prompts, but they are not from a place of frustration. They are from a place of "I know you'll get this"; I can love you where you are *and* I can find a place within me that enjoys where you are in your learning right now.

It is the same with our partners.

In this metaphor you are the light (energy), the glorious golden beaming light of the sun; he is as a flower (the one searching for the energy). In order for the flower (him) to face the sun (you), the sun **does not**:

- Yell to the flower "This way! Over here!"
- Tell the flower where it is
- Snap the flower's head off trying to turn it
- Uproot the flower and do the moving *for* it

The sun shines brilliantly with the full force of her life-energy and waits for the flower (her lover) to orient towards her. The sun does not second-guess the flower's ability to orient towards its light. It trusts it will, in its own divine timing. It is the same in our relationship.

Get on the same team. You are not on opposite teams.
What do you need to get onto the same team about this one next "situation"?

You may have different roles within the team, but the team is working towards a united goal.
What do you need to do this? What does he need?

Consider if you are complicit in the creation of this current situation? If there's anything you can clue him in on?

Uplevel your communication

Tip 1

If you have a mountain more at home in his masculine, asking him *how do you feel about that?* asks him to get into his **feminine** polarity. He will either need a lot of time to make that shift or he won't be feeling "I don't really feel anything about it" – he's in his masculine "thinking."

Shift your question to *Okay, what do you **think** about that?* – likely, this will ensure an answer.

If you're asking him to *feel* and move across to the feminine pole, know that *you* in return will need to take up the masculine pole. **Be aware of what you are asking** before you decide you're disappointed with the response. Which polarity do you want to take up? Which polarity do you want him to take up? Choose your question accordingly.

Tip 2

If you have a mountain more at home in his feminine than his masculine, *How do you feel?* will be effortless for him to answer. He may indeed be an exceptional communicator, able to feel and flow with ease. Which is great, if *you* prefer to be the mountain most of the time.

However, if it is *not* how you wish to feel in this moment, then *you* must take up the flower pole and be responsible for feeling and energy-flow. Your questions need to change form in order to "push" him back into his mountain state. *How do you feel* becomes *What do you think? What do you see as possible directions? What do **you** think we should do?*

Every time he avoids answering with leadership and decision and instead seeks to defer to *your* direction and guidance, you must avoid the temptation to give "your two cents worth" and instead hold your feminine polarity, giving him time (practice) to orient into his masculine.

If he says *I don't know; Whatever you think* or *I just feel* ... you only respond with "I feel" sentences or with questions that elicit his decision:

Him: What do you want for dinner tonight?
You: I don't know, what do you want?

Him: Whatever you want.
You: I don't know what I feel like. What do you think?

Him: I think I want whatever you want.
You: I don't know what I want. What are my options?

Him: Chinese, pizza, pasta, fish and chips. What do you want?
You: I don't know ... (feel into what you desire to be filled with).

Give him the *opportunity* to lead forward movement, direction and decisions. Hand over being the leader to him, for just a short while. Even if it's not what you end up doing, let him and you practise.

Let him work it out for himself. Let him be uncomfortable. This is good masculine practice. Avoid your temptation to offer support and "buffer" his discomfort by offering comfort. Just stay open and in loving connection.

When he does offer a decision, don't shoot him down. Recognise that he's attempting to establish a new way of meeting you, love *that* even if you can't love his suggestion.

It's like the childhood game of "hot and cold." Do you remember that?

You hide an object and as your friend moves around trying to find it, you offer guidance: "warmer," "cooler," "OOO! Hot!" "Nope. Cold" ... and on it goes until they find the precious item ... which you know they will *AND* you enjoy their attempts at guessing. It is the same with our partners, only it gets to be sexier!

Him: Chinese?
You, slight frown, low energy: Hmmm ...

Him: Fish and chips?
You, low animated response: Hmmmm ...

Him: Gourmet burgers?
You, excitedly: Oh yes! That's exactly what I want! Thank you! (big kiss and exuberant hug, possibly some cheerleader style jumping).

Don't get lost in feminine-rejection stories of *This is ridiculous. Why should I have to do this? It feels unnatural.* This is why you're *both* practising! It *will* feel uncomfortable before it feels part of your repertoire, before "staged" turns into "delighted."

You're learning to sit in your feminine again; he's learning to guide in his masculine again. Equally challenging practice, equal self-ownership required.

Tip 3

Behind every "you" statement is an "I crave" statement.

If you stop at the projection *You're* ... you miss the message from your heart.

Every time you want to make a "you" statement, pause long enough to ask yourself:

What am I really craving?
What am I afraid of?
What do I yearn to feel?

Let these answers guide your relationship conversations.

Likely you're just desiring something you haven't openly acknowledged yet!

For example:
You statement: "You always choose your work or study or hobbies. You don't spend time with us. You're selfish."

Realisation after journaling on questions: "I crave to choose myself first in the same way he does. I've been putting my needs and desires last and guilting myself for time away from parenting. I miss his attention on me."

I statement: "I've realised I miss spending time with you; when can we do something together? I'm really hurting about not getting to the gym/my art class and I've only just realised how important this is to me. Can we sit down and work out how to fit it in to our week?"

Tip 4
Your best tool in relationship is curiosity: "Tell me more …" If you're ever unclear, ask for clarity.

Get targeted

It is my hope you have dog-eared, underlined and written notes throughout this book. I want you to feel capable of taking yourself from where you are to where you want to be. Don't scattergun your approach, get targeted: *where do you need to focus your practice right now?* Keep it real, keep it in integrity and honesty, don't try to bypass or pole-vault your way to a perceived end-line; you'll shock yourself backwards or break something in the process. The micro-progression steps you take are the most pattern changing and life altering.

Track your changes with **tangible** goals. Try a three-, six- or twelve-month goal. After you've created the relationship and sexuality vision and long-term goals you are both aligned with, and you're on the same team, work out the micro-progression-steps to getting there.

> *We've had a chat about our relationship goals, he seemed really energised at the end of that chat. We're aiming for two date nights a week but not always meeting it. Maybe one a week is a more achievable goal to start with. We're both super excited about our future together and that's largely because of the insights and tools I've learnt from here.*
>
> – Elyse

Break each goal down:
- What needs to change?
- How can we break this push/pull, connection/disconnection cycle we are in?
- What do we each need to be able to do that?
- What needs to be added in?
- What wants to be explored?
- What would this look like as a monthly, weekly, daily action

plan or goal?

- Ask each other. Take it in turns, until you're both super pumped to do this together!

Celebrate your mini-successes. Acknowledge the smallest shifts, for they create the huge ones, and what you appreciate, appreciates. If you don't celebrate yourself, you'll miss the opportunity to see how far you've come and the motivation to keep going. Remember, he chose YOU, all of you; it's a disservice and minimising to deny both of you that experience. Just know, his shift IS your shift too; the outer is always a reflection of the inner. Celebrate your shifts, however small.

> *There is nothing like unblocking a kitchen sink at 1am in the morning that makes you realise how far your relationship has come. No tears, no tantrums, just tired cooperation and appreciation for each other. We paused, exhausted, over a pile of still dirty dishes and the realisation that we needed a plumber.*
>
> *Hubby: we've handled this really well together. Imagine if we'd tried to do this before Julie's work.*
>
> *– Cathy*

You are worth celebrating, individually and as a couple.

Conclusion

You're here. You made it. Reading what my heart and soul want *you* to carry forwards. I love you already. There's now a piece of my heart intertwined with yours, and I know I'll meet you at that intersection. Thank you. Thank you for trusting yourself enough to say "yes" to reading this book, to spending your precious time and space with me. Thank you for trusting me to guide a small piece of your journey.

I hope your feminine reclamation becomes the most potent self-care practice you've ever had.

And remember: a queen never rules alone. She can do hard and great things *with* a support crew; please find the women who will fan your flames and support your journey into embodied living.

May you find the ecstasy you were born to experience.
May you realise the grace that was always yours.
May you walk with love behind you, and in front of you.
May you feel blessings like blossoms in a summer breeze as the kiss of the Goddess, saying "thank you" for expressing her truth and presence on this earth.
You are wildly healing.

Along the way, don't forget to be generous. It is easy to find fault in another; far harder to own the "not so kind" reflection of ourselves and habituated ways we show up. For everything you want *him* to change, what is the equal and opposite change *you* will make?

Be generous with each other. Be generous with yourself as you navigate "unlearning" old patterns and insert new ways of being. Like learning to read, be patient. Don't quit, collapse and close up shop. How long can you hold your polarity for? Is 20 seconds with no reaction *it*?? Is that really what you and your desired relationship are worth? Can you hold it for 15 minutes? Thirty minutes? Can you practise every day?

You're learning a new language. Give yourself time, patience and compassion; and spread a little of that to your partner, who you've changed the rules on after years of training.

Don't wish you were more the same. Desire exists in opposites. Worship the different ways you each belong to this world and function best. Give each other the gifts of your own innate polarity and receive its complementary opposite with as much grace.

Remember, your partner is your best teacher, but it's never about making changes for them. It's always about YOU. The moment you understand energy in your body, its amplification, and send it out for him to receive is the moment he notices, but it will feel most magnificent and powerful for *you*.

Don't get stuck in your head that *I'm doing all of this hard work for you and you're doing nothing* ... You're doing all of this for YOU, regardless of what it means or doesn't mean for him. This hard stuff is here for you to learn. Intimacy and all its awkwardness offer you your greatest opening and expansion.

It is my hope, prayer, and heart's yearning that you'll "leave it all on the dancefloor." Risk it all and claim it all. I want to live in a world where women, like you, like me, are lit up from the inside out. Luminous beings, claiming their *own* light and shining that light on whatever they choose to bless in this moment. You are light. You are life. You are energy. You are love.

May you fill your house with flowers,
taste honey dripping from your lips.

May you want for more:
more love, deeper love, unfathomable love.

May you want for this flesh to unfold
with the softness of rose petals.

May you be soothed by rain,
blown open by wind
and seduced by the sun.

May you dance in the centre of your flower,
let pollen stick this moment to your flesh.

May you gather the nectar of so many experiences,
it flavours the honey you make.

May you leave this body *in* love,
Knowing you left it *all* on the dance floor.
You didn't hold back.
You didn't choose fear and closure over love and opening.

May you want for flowers and mountains,
and find bees and honey.

All my love,
Jules xx

For my children,

Please know, my loves, love exists all around you. Don't give up on love, ever. Even when you're hurt. Especially when you're hurt. Return to love, again and again. Do not mistake human romanticised love for soul-love. The divine brings us love in *all* its shades; the soul seeks love to guide our growth. Often our revelations are born out of pain. Look for the lesson, seek the growth. It's all *on* the way, not *in* the way. Awaken what love guides you towards.

May you have the courage to leap, falling into faith because you have trust in *your own* heart and a proven inner, knowing that you'll build your wings on the way.

May your relationships be as deeply fulfilling as ours is and was, and may you know how to guide it when it falls short. Love, honour and respect lead to an exceptional life. Go create yours. May love fill the pages of your life's journey.

Soul-deep love and gratitude,
Mum xx

Where to go to connect with more of Julie's work:

It is my hearts desire you take this knowledge deeper into your life and relationship. The spaces I create are for women who want to be loved better by becoming better lovers. Let me teach you how to move into greater feminine flow, love with generosity and open yourself with deeper reverence and sensation; the result is electric chemistry and desire!

Honey, you've got this.
You can do hard things, with support.
You can create huge shifts, with sweet motivation.

If you've exited this temple and you're ready for more, please connect with me:

Web	www.julietenner.love
Facebook	@lovejulietenner
Instagram	@julietenner.love
YouTube	Julie Tenner

Here's the spaces I offer for your growth, empowerment and embodiment:

HONEY CLUB – *Relationship, Embodiment, Feminine Practice membership group.* Honey Club is a space of weekly integration and practice to remember, awaken, stay motivated and keep learning and growing.

QUEEN SCHOOL – *10-week relationship transformation program dedicated to evoking the love you crave within yourself and your lover.* Learn how to be loved better by becoming a better lover, guided by me and supported by women just like you.

COACHING – *1:1 space.* An intimate warm cocoon where we can delve into what holds you back, heal what you've carried for too long and create a unique practice for you, so you can love without guardedness and create the life or experience you want with intention and confidence.

Connect with me through Nourishing The Mother Podcast:
Search "Nourishing the Mother" on your podcast app.

Web	www.nourishingthemother.com.au
Facebook	@nourishingthemother
Instagram	@nourishingthemother
YouTube	Nourishing The Mother

Lightning Source UK Ltd.
Milton Keynes UK
UKHW041833010421
381389UK00003B/926